The Heyday of

BR STANDARD LOCOMOTIVES

PAUL LEAVENS & SVMRC

Once again we dedicate this album to those photographers of the railway scene of any era – thanks gentlemen!

ISBN 978-1-913049-02-7

Printed and bound by The Amadeus Press, Cleckheaton,West Yorkshire

Published by Book Law Publications, 382 Carlton Hill, Nottingham, NG4 1JA

Introduction

When it was decided to construct 999 steam locomotives to represent what was to become British Railway's Standard types the classes chosen numbered twelve different designs in total. Those designs utilised wheel arrangements which were already in common use by the 'Big Four' railway companies with three classes having the 4-6-2 Pacific arrangement. Two offered the tried, tested and very popular 4-6-0 layout whilst three more used yet another well used type, the 2-6-0. The three tank engine classes used just two wheel arrangements: the popular 2-6-4 and the Prairie type 2-6-2. Finally we revert back to the tender engines and the final – twelfth – class which brought in a new and somewhat radical wheel arrangement for the United Kingdom and into production for the first time: 2-10-0. The last of the Standard designs to appear, the 9F was BR's answer to moving heavy freight over the system be it slow moving mineral slogs, fitted mineral trains, perishable goods trains, or as things worked out the occasional express passenger train and certainly seasonal excursion workings.

So, the scene was set and BR required every last one of the engines at least for a short while. Circumstances in the United Kingdom were changing much faster than Government had envisaged. Social conditions were being changed voluntarily and forcibly. The public had more money they wanted and demanded better conditions. They had as one Prime Minister noted 'Never had it so good' and it was true. Public transport was suddenly second choice. Personal transport in the shape of the family car for those who could afford them became an overnight hit. Road transport haulage companies sprang up everywhere when Government relaxed what restrictions had been in place. The result saw BR slowly fall apart, not helped by self-serving and corrupt Government ministers. The body that ran the railways were inept, toothless, and were only in it, it seemed, to get a free lunch after the Friday board meetings, not to mention the retainers for turning-up!

What chance for the 999 new steam locomotives which were designed to get BR through a difficult period? None is the answer. To borrow some words from a famous title penned some twenty-odd years ago and which had nothing at all to do with railways, this tome or perhaps more correctly its subject could be described as having 'A Brief History in Time!'

(*Front Cover*) Class 4 No.75074 at Reading shed, 10th November 1964. *Paul Leavens.*

(*Rear Cover top*) Class 3 2-6-2T No.82006 Nine Elms, 5th March 1966. *Paul Leavens.*

(*Rear Cover bottom*) Class 5 No.73119 working empty carriage stock at Clapham Junction on 25th May 1961. *Paul Leavens.*

1: CLASS 7 4-6-2 - The 'Britannia's.'

Eastern Region – The former Great Eastern Lines of the ER were desperate for suitable motive power to handle the accelerated expresses planned for the services out of Liverpool Street station. The Britannia Pacifics embodied all of BR's hope, aspirations, expectations, and European steam locomotive design. The class was borne from a requirement whereby steam locomotives could run to express timings using inferior coal. Maintenance was to be made easier and therefore quicker by building access into the design. That the responsible draughtsmen managed to create a good looking and well balanced locomotive is a tribute to their understanding and skills. Of course it wasn't just the ER GE lines which were due for a face lift some other areas too were due for some new motive power. The first fifteen Class 7 Pacifics were designated for the ER and Crewe managed to deliver Nos.70000 to 70014 during the first six months of 1951, the first BR Standard locomotives for a worn-out railway system. Besides the initial fifteen, the GE lines received Nos.70035 to 70044 which were again spread between Norwich and Stratford except that the last two went on loan almost immediately to the LM Region at Longsight and never ventured onto the ER as 9A became their permanent home at least until September 1961 (70043) and December 1958 (70044). So there we have the ER Britannia's set up for a lifetime of express passenger work but then came a couple of hiccups! The first problem, which was to show itself within weeks of the class entering service, involved water getting into cylinders by way of the steam intake. Various modifications cured that one. However during their first summer in service certain engines started to show signs of their coupled wheels shifting on the axle and at least four engines displayed the problem. It was deemed by authority to be so serious that all of those locomotives in service – some twenty-five at the end of October 1951 – were withdrawn pending investigations and modifications. It is not the intention of this tome to deal with the cause or aftermath of this particular problem but it was sorted and the locomotives returned to service forthwith.

No.70035 departs from Liverpool Street on an unknown date – autumn judging by the attire of the adoring crowds – showing it had plenty of steam available. The boilers of these 7P rated Pacifics were equipped with those wide fireboxes which were built to burn anything which came out of the ground. However, the ER authorities at Stratford ensured that their 'Brits' got the best of the coal on offer anyway with Norwich also getting its share. *Paul Leavens.*

Norwich shared the East Anglia express work with Stratford and 32A's No.70035 RUDYARD KIPLING is at the latter shed in 1960 turned, serviced and ready to return to Norfolk. One of the second batch sent to the ER, this Pacific was delivered in December 1952 to Norwich but it also did a couple of stints at March with the last one in June 1963 seeing the engine transferred to Kingmoor. *D.H.Beecroft*.

An undated view of No.70038 ROBIN HOOD at Stratford shed probably shortly after delivery in January 1953. It was February 1959 before this engine transferred to Norwich but that event coincided with the arrival of the Type 4 diesels on the GE lines. October 1960 saw 'the outlaw' moving on again, this time to March. A year later it was off to Immingham and then in December 1963 to Carlisle with the end now in sight! *Chris Dunne*.

(*above*) No.70038 heading an express at Liverpool Street circa 1956! *Paul Leavens*.

(*below*) Starting life as one of the ER batch at Norwich at the end of May 1951, No.70013 OLIVER CROMWELL spent the next twelve years and seven months working the principal expresses around East Anglia, north to York on the Colchester-Newcastle express on occasion, and often on the Harwich boat trains to Sheffield – the erstwhile named *THE NORTH COUNTRY CONTINENTAL* – where electric traction would take over for the trans-Pennine section of the journey. Like the others on the Eastern, they just got on with what they were given and nobody really took any particular member of the class as being special or otherwise. A transfer to March depot on 10th September 1961 marked the end of the engines' involvement with hauling any expresses out of Liverpool Street but other expresses still required their services. By the end of 1961 all of the ER contingent were resident at 31B; the diesels had arrived on the region and the 'Brits' were on their way to pastures anew. No.70013 was transferred out of the region in December 1963 and sent to Carlisle Kingmoor on the 1st via Newcastle; sisters 70002, 70003, 70006, 70007, 70008, 70009, 70011, 70035, and 70036 all followed, many of them after a period in store at March depot. Our subject engine was allocated to both Kingmoor and Upperby until 9th January 1968 when it was sent to Carnforth, a somewhat unusual transfer considering all of the surviving 'Brits' were congregated at Kingmoor. However, that single movement proved to be quite significant in that OLIVER CROMWELL would end up as one of the small bunch of surviving steam locomotives as BR drew the curtains on steam traction. On 16th June 1968 the Pacific was photographed beneath the coaling plant at Carnforth looking fairly reasonable but not quite ready for the big day in August. Note the nameplates had been removed. *David Dalton*.

No.70012 JOHN OF GAUNT working an RCTS enthusiasts' special at Nottingham (Midland) on 2nd October 1965. The 'Brit' was allocated to Crewe South shed at the time after joining the LM Region in April 1963 at Willesden. Of all the fifty-five members of the class this particular locomotive probably had some of the more colourful allocations to add to its quota with Yarmouth (South Town), and Llandudno Junction besides the more usual locations. *David Dalton.*

March based No.70037 HEREWARD THE WAKE has charge of a Colchester-Newcastle express passing through Doncaster on the Down main in 1961. The 'Brit' would work as far as York where a North Eastern Region engine would take over unless of course there was a failure at York then No.70037 would work through. The sight of these engines in Newcastle was something of a rarity when they were allocated to the ER but after the almost en masse transfer to Carlisle they became regular visitors to Tyneside. Doncaster of course was quite used to these engines as all of the ER batch was overhauled at The Plant works from the mid-1950s until the end of 1961. *SVMRC.*

London Midland Region - The LMR's first 'Brit' was No.70015 which went new to Camden on 12th June 1951 but was on loan from the Western Region. At the end of 1951 it went to the ER at Stratford also on loan; it eventually reached the WR on 17th May 1953. The next new engine to join the region was No.70030 which went to Holyhead in November 1952 along with No.70031; 70032 and 70033 followed in December. All four of the Holyhead quartet had transferred to Longsight by the end of the following January and they were greeted in Manchester by No.70034 which had arrived at 9A on 20th December. It was another eighteen months before Crewe sent any more to the LMR when No.70045 arrived in Holyhead in June 1954. The as yet un-named 70045 was the first engine of the last batch of the class and had been given a different tender to the previous engines of the class which were all coupled to either BR1 or BR1A a slightly modified version of BR1. The new tender was a BR1D which was heavier than the others with a two tons greater coal capacity and 500 gallons more water than BR1. All subsequent new engines were coupled to the BR1D tenders. No.70046 was next and that too went to Holyhead in July 1954 along with 70047 and 70048. No.70049 arrived in Anglesey during August to complete what was now a Holyhead quintet. However, none of the other four were as yet named so some of the magic might not have been totally in place for 6J but all was not lost because in July 1957 No.70045 was named LORD ROWALLAN; 70048 became THE TERRITORIAL ARMY 1908-1958 from 23rd July 1958; 70046 was named ANZAC during September 1959 and 70049 was not named until long after leaving Holyhead for Chester in December 1959. No.70047 was never named – LANCASHIRE & YORKSHIRE was lined up for this engine but the event did not take place – and also transferred to Chester in December 1959.

In a previous life this 'Brit' was a Knight of the Realm and worked on the ER but now it's just a Pacific working from Kingmoor in unlined green livery. No.70041's eleven year journey to Carlisle took in the following depots: Stratford 20th March 1953 new; Norwich in February 1959; Immingham December 1960; Upperby December 1963; Kingmoor January 1964. *Paul Leavens*.

No.70021 residing in the works at Crewe on an unknown date shortly after the removal of the MORNING STAR nameplates! A 9B Stockport Edgeley shed plate is affixed to the smokebox door so the date must have been anywhere between May 1966 and June 1967 when it transferred (should that be gravitated?) to Kingmoor. Another ex-WR engine, No.70021 started its career at Laira in August 1951 where for five years she climbed those Devon banks whilst working express passenger trains. A transfer to Canton in January 1957 saw Cardiff having its services for just eighteen months because on 12th July 1958 she was loaned to Trafford Park shed to work the Manchester (Central) – London (St Pancras) expresses. Obviously a success over the difficult route through the Peak District, No.70021 was transferred to 9E on a permanent basis a week later! Other 'Brits' came to Trafford Park during that period – No.70017 ARROW was already there – 70014 IRON DUKE and 70015 APOLLO came too. MORNING STAR moved away to Willesden in February 1961 followed by a three shed shuffle in 1965 – Crewe North, South, and Newton Heath in that order! Withdrawal took place at Kingmoor on 30th December 1967. *Paul Leavens.*

It was once named VULCAN but by the time it was working this Up express through Preston in 1967 it had lost those nameplates. No.70024 was the last of the 1951 build and it emerged from Crewe on 6th October just in time to be withdrawn because of the roller-bearing problem with the shifting wheels affecting other members of the class. Destined for the WR when new, No.70024 was in limbo at Swindon for a number of months before finally being allocated to Laira in February 1953. It was loaned to the SR for a couple of months from May 1953 at Exmouth Junction but was returned to Plymouth in July. In December 1956 it joined most of the other WR 'Brits' at Canton where until the end of 1961 status quo reigned. Starting at Aston in October 1961, No.70024 served at ten more LMR sheds before withdrawal from Kingmoor on the penultimate day of 1967 – in actuality the engine was at Speke Junction when the hammer fell. *Paul Leavens.*

No.70022 is made ready for a ride on the Crewe South turntable in late 1965. *Paul Leavens.*

No.70042 LORD ROBERTS pauses at Derby with a late morning Manchester (Central) to London (St Pancras) express in 1960 when this 'Brit' was allocated to Trafford Park simply to work these passenger trains. By the end of the year the engine had transferred to Willesden whilst Nos.70031, 70032, and 70033 transferred in to keep the expresses within the times until the Type 4 'Peak' diesel-electrics took over. *SVMRC*.

After all its trials and tribulations with the Mechanical & Electrical Engineer from Derby since the summer of 1953, No.70044 returned to a somewhat normal lifestyle working express passenger trains from Longsight shed. On an unrecorded date in March 1957 the engine had just brought empty stock into Manchester (London Road) station for an Up working into platform 4 and now that has gone the Pacific was free to run to the end of the platform and run across the station throat to take up the 0935 working to Euston - *THE MANCUNIAN* - which was in platform 6. It would require some smart handling by all concerned as the time was already 0920. Note however that the relevant lamps are already in place. *SVMRC.*

No.70044 ready for the 'off' at London Road in March 1957. *SVMRC.*

When the migration to Carlisle was almost complete! No.70003 JOHN BUNYAN – complete in every respect – runs through Hilton Junction south of Perth with an early afternoon fish train from Aberdeen on 27th August 1964. The Pacific had transferred from March, after a period in store there, during the previous Christmas. *Paul Leavens*.

Scottish Region – The Scottish Region was not only the last region to receive a quota of Britannia's it also received the smallest number of them. In August 1954 Nos.70050 FIRTH OF CLYDE and 70051 FIRTH OF FORTH were sent to Polmadie to join the Stanier Pacifics which were already plying up and down the West Coast main line. No.70052 FIRTH OF TAY followed on the 21st whilst 70053 MORAY FIRTH arrived in September along with 70054 DORNOCH FIRTH. There was another with a Scottish theme name – 70049 SOLWAY FIRTH – but that name was not applied until May 1960 some six years after the engine entered service. As things turned out, No.70049 never worked from any Scottish shed anyway although Kingmoor was close enough in those latter years. For the record No.70049 was considered for the name FURNESS which might have been more appropriate? Now the five Scottish 'Brits' worked from 66A until April 1962 in the case of Nos.70050, 70051, and 70052 and October 1958 for Nos.70053 and 70054. All of them went to English sheds eventually with the first three going to Crewe North via six months at Corkerhill whereas the last pair went direct to Holbeck until September 1962 when they too went to 5A. All five had been involved with passenger workings over the G&SWR main line and the S&C line from Leeds to St Enoch, and then the diesels came. After 1962 they went everywhere; North Wales; GCR main line; and the WCML north of Crewe. They all came to Kingmoor from where they were withdrawn and all five ended up in Scottish scrapyards.

Happy days! No.70051 FIRTH OF FORTH at Polmadie not too long after arrival from Crewe. The name plates of all five of the Polmadie engines were fitted at St Rollox the day following the engines arrival at 66A. The tenders coupled to the Scottish engines were the BR1D type the heaviest of the three types coupled to the Britannia's (BR1, BR1A, BR1D) at 54 tons 10 cwt which equated to 4,725 gallons of water, and 9 tons of coal. *D.H.Beecroft.*

No date, no name, and no hope! No.70053 at Kingmoor with sister engines awaiting the inevitable. *D.H.Beecroft*.

The business end of Crewe North's No.70050 at Willesden 18th October 1963. *Paul Leavens*.

Southern Region - The SR never received any new 'Britannia's' but they did have a couple of engines which they made special and which were kept for one particular job – hauling the Up and Down services of the *GOLDEN ARROW* between Victoria, Dover and Folkestone. No.70004 WILLIAM SHAKESPEARE arrived at Stewarts Lane shed on the last day of September 1951 when it was some six months old. The Pacific remained at 73A until 21st June 1958 when it transferred to the LMR at Kentish Town. No.70014 IRON DUKE was introduced to the Southern three months earlier when it transferred to Nine Elms on 10th June 1951 from Norwich. In September it was resident at Stewarts Lane as a turn-about engine with sister 70004 working that special Pullman service. It too left the region on 21st June 1958 for Kentish Town and a less pampered existence. There had been others – 70009 to 71A from May to September 1951; 70017 and 70023 Salisbury summer 1953 on loan; 70024, 70028 and 70029 to Exmouth Junction summer 1953 on loan from WR – which had fleeting relationships with the region but the two aforementioned take-the-biscuit!

(*above*) With a Down service of the *GOLDEN ARROW* No.70014 IRON DUKE is somewhere on the Southern in 1953. There is a possibility that someone in the BR hierarchy requested this engine to work the train especially for all the French visitors arriving in London to note the name as they left the platform at Victoria. There is a rumour that somebody wanted to bring these boat trains into Waterloo but that never happened; only Winston Churchill got his wish to have Waterloo station as the departure point for his funeral train even though its destination was in Oxfordshire. *Paul Leavens*.

(*below*) Working hard, No.70014 again with another Down service at another unidentified location in 1953. *Paul Leavens*.

Western Region – The Western Region's first new Britannia was No.70015 APPOLLO which like sister No.70016 ARIEL never actually ran on WR metals until May 1953 almost two years after they left the works at Crewe. The reason for their late arrival stemmed from the fact that both had been out on loan both initially to the LMR and then the ER although at different engine sheds. However, they got to the WR eventually with 70015 going to Old Oak Common and 70016 to Laira. Meanwhile, in their absence, the WR had been receiving Nos.70017 to 70024 between June and October 1951 a period which coincided with the coupled wheel/axle/roller bearing problem which then saw all of them temporarily withdrawn. Laira and Old Oak Common sheds were affected but by February 1952 everything was back to normal. The next batch – 70025 to 70029 – were part of the 1952-build and they arrived in late 1952 to complete the Western Region allocation of fifteen engines. None of them finished their careers on the region and most had moved to the LM Region by late 1961 and in some cases as early as July 1958. It wasn't really a case of the Britannia Pacifics not quite fitting in but more of a 'Here come the diesels so what shall we get rid of first?' Last in, first out!

No.70029 SHOOTING STAR stabled alongside the rebuilt shed at Cardiff Canton on 12th August 1956. Note the original condition smoke deflectors with the handrail which was to play a major part in a future accident with a sister engine. *David Dalton.*

(*above*) Undated, this image of No.70028 ROYAL STAR shows the Pacific at Swindon minus tender and in the company of the Lickey banker No.92079 at some time in 1959. *Paul Leavens.*

(*below*) No.70028 heading an Up afternoon express at Potters Bar on 31st May 1963. At this time the Pacific was allocated to Aston so why it was working on the ECML north of London is unknown to this writer. The stock looks vaguely ER so may not be a diverted train. No.70028 was transferred to Willesden a few days later but this method of transfer via another region seems highly unusual! *Paul Leavens.*

(*above*) Willesden 1st May 1964: 1A did a good job with No.70020 MERCURY when they had it from June 1963 ex-Carlisle Canal to January 1965 when Crewe North took it on. I wager that it never looked like this again! *Paul Leavens.*

(*below*) No.70025 WESTERN STAR – shades of Swindon's naming madness here? – stands beneath the coaling plant at Camden shed on 13th July 1963. *Paul Leavens.*

(*above*) Perhaps there was a phantom cleaner doing the rounds at Willesden. This is No.70021 MORNING STAR on 21st July 1963. *Paul Leavens*.

(*below*) Shortly after transfer to Willesden from March shed No.70034 THOMAS HARDY has charge of an Up WCML express and is running over Bushey troughs on 27th July 1963 without dipping the scoop. *Paul Leavens*.

And, to finish off the class we present a little montage of three engines during their final days: No.70002 GEOFFREY CHAUCER was letting the banker do the work on Shap 1st August 1964. *Paul Leavens*.

We haven't done much on freight yet so here is No.70018 FLYING DUTCHMAN making friends at South Kirkton on 26th July 1963 whilst working a Down freight. *Paul Leavens*.

No.70031 BYRON does pick-up some water from Bushey troughs during the late afternoon of 27th July 1963. Working Up express 1A35, the Pacific was now part of Willesden's stud but had spent most of its life in Manchester working from Longsight for seven and a half years and Trafford Park for nearly two and a half. TENNYSON and CHARLES DICKENS followed suit! *Paul Leavens*.

2: CLASS 8P 4-6-2 'DUKE OF GLOUCESTER'

No.71000 at Crewe works before it was hauled away to South Wales. The removal of the cylinders and associated valve gear is plain to see. There followed a period of purgatory at Barry and then along came a bunch of believers – some called them 'nutters' – who invested time, money and know-how into resurrecting what should have been in a former life the most powerful passenger locomotive on BR but somebody had got a few simple things wrong in the design and the 8P was damned for its whole BR existence. In preservation the locomotive has proved its credentials and is today a tribute to all the hard work and dedication lavished on a superb example of British engineering. *Chris Dunne.*

Another view of 71000 at Crewe with A4 No.60026 changing ends on 2nd April 1967. *David Dalton.*

3: CLASS 6 4-6-2 - The 'Clans.'

What more can we say about the 'Clans' which hasn't already been written? The answer is not a lot but we can just point out that the ten engines which made up the class were all built at Crewe and were initially maintained there. That they were split equally between two different sheds, in two different countries, and that they were divided equally to be scrapped at BR works and private scrap yards was probably more down to the fact that they were built in an even number – ten! However, although the two depots that housed them had the same origins in the Caledonian Railway, they were treated very differently by the two establishments with one – Polmadie – having seemingly nothing but disregard for their batch whilst the other shed – Kingmoor – used and treated them with a respect of sorts and indeed probably got the best out of them? Appearing at the end of 1951 the first two – 72000 and 72001 – were allocated to Polmadie followed in January and February 1952 by Nos.72002, 72003, and 72004. Nos.72005–72009 were all delivered to Kingmoor during February and March 1952. Intended as replacements for 'Jubilee' 4-6-0s the engines settled down to typical workings which took them south of the border with passenger and parcels trains from Glasgow to Preston – it was intended to use them on Manchester and Liverpool expresses from Glasgow but coal capacity became an issue and only those working from Carlisle were entrusted to work south of Preston. Of course Kingmoor was part of the Scottish Region when the class was delivered which essentially keeps our 'survey' fairly tidy as regards BR Standard locomotives.

Kingmoor's No.72009 CLAN STEWART heads an Up parcels train over Beattock summit on 27th March 1964. The external condition of the engine was simply typical of the period; No.72009 still had another seventeen months of operational use in front of it before withdrawal on 28th August 1965 as the penultimate member of the class. *Paul Leavens.*

No.72009 again, but sometime later on 1st August 1964 working a northbound train over Beattock with the aid of a steam banker. Note the external condition of the Pacific. This was one of three Kingmoor engines which went out into the big wide world in 1957 and 1958; Nos.72005 and 72006 went to Haymarket in November 1957 for a six-month period whereas our subject here went to Stratford for a period of working over the former Great Eastern lines during October to December 1958. *Paul Leavens*.

Kingmoor's batch remained extremely active until some major mechanical problem took each of them gradually out of the running. This is No.72006 CLAN MACKENZIE with an express for Perth at Gleneagles on Friday 28th August 1964. This engine succumbed on 21st May 1965 but didn't leave Kingmoor for its new owners' premises – in Shettleston – until 11th August 1966. *Paul Leavens*.

(*above*) Stripped of its plates, No.72006 was stored in the leaking shed at Dumfries on 6th April 1966. *Paul Leavens*.

(*below*) Some detail of No.72003 CLAN FRASER, albeit with bits missing. The cylinder information is just a little small to read. *Paul Leavens*.

Although undated, this image of No.72003 CLAN FRASER at Polmadie throws some light on the approximate date with a chalked legend on the smokebox door stating 'Blast pipe OK 11/6/59' with other references about the cylinders. The Pacific was at home having some work done on the cylinders and must have been awaiting parts having been pushed out into the yard along with an unidentified 'Princess Royal'. *Paul Leavens*.

No.72003 at Kingmoor whilst en route to the BR works at Darlington in September 1963 for cutting-up. Withdrawn en masse with sisters 72000, 72001, 72002, and 72004 on 29th December 1962 (for the record Nos.72000 and 72001 were officially received at 66A on 29th December 1954) and lay derelict at various locations in the Scottish Region until removed to Darlington during September 1963. All five were cut up by the middle of February 1964. *Paul Leavens*.

Stripped of its nameplates and adorned with the yellow stripe on the cab side No.72006 is seen on the ash pit at Kingmoor shed during its final days in the spring of 1965. Ironically if there was ever a class less likely to venture south of Crewe during this period it was unknown to this writer. *Paul Leavens*.

Happier times for steam, No.72000 CLAN BUCHANAN approaches Carnforth at speed with a combined Manchester and Liverpool to Glasgow express which it has brought from Preston circa 1960. *SVMRC.*

No.72009 under the wires at Colchester in November 1958! Note not an electrification warning flash plate anywhere on the engine! Whatever the reason for sending the Pacific south to the GE lines, it was soon returned from whence it came. *SVMRC.*

4: CLASS 5 4-6-0

General – Amongst the first of the Standard classes into production, the one-hundred and seventy-two Class 5 4-6-0s were also amongst the last with No.73000 appearing from Derby works in April 1951 and 73154 being put into traffic in June 1957, also ex-Derby shops; the last engine numerically – 73171 – had entered traffic a month beforehand ex-Doncaster. All of BR's regions were allocated varying numbers of these engines with the Eastern getting just five, the Western ten, the North Eastern a dozen, Southern Region twenty-three, Scottish Region sixty-five, and the LM Region sixty-seven. Just two BR workshops were involved in building the class – Derby and Doncaster – with the former establishment turning out one hundred and thirty examples.

No.73035 stables at Eastfield shed in September 1965 after a visit to Cowlairs where the lined green livery first applied by Swindon works during the summer of 1959 was spruced-up. Now a Patricroft engine, having transferred from Shrewsbury in July 1965, No.73035 started life as one of the Scottish Region allocation 73030-73039 listed as allocated to Polmadie (for some reason alternate engines 73031, 73033, 73035, 73037, and 73039 were to become 66A engines, whereas 73030, 73032, 73024, 73036, and 73038 were listed for Kingmoor!) but no sooner had the early engines reached Scotland than they were transferred away to Shrewsbury or at least Nos.73033 to 73037 were. The others were sent to: 73030 Rugby Testing Station via CM&EE Derby; 73031 Derby; 73032 and 73039 St Philips Marsh; 73038 Chester West. They never did return to work from sheds in Scotland but ironically 73035 did manage a visit to Cowlairs and a little running-in from 65A. *D.H.Beecroft.*

No.73035 again but by now on this first day of May 1962 she is allocated to 89A Shrewsbury. Posing in the late morning sunshine, the Cl.5 is on Stafford shed yard with Rugby based Stanier 5 No.44760 being serviced. No.73035 had just worked in from Shrewsbury via Wellington. The engine would end its days in January 1968 on the LM Region proper at Patricroft where good company awaited. *David Dalton.*

A close-up of the business end of Caprotti equipped No.73143 at Patricroft in 1967. This engine was a latecomer to the spiritual home of the Caprotti Class 5s having arrived in February 1964 from Rowsley; prior to that it had spent the whole of its previous eight years at various LM sheds. 9H proved to be its last and it was withdrawn there in August 1967. This image must have been recorded after that withdrawal date as the locomotive is ready for a one-way journey to a scrapyard! *Paul Leavens.*

(*above*) The usual Patricroft finish! Note the very neat rendition of PATRICROFT on the bufferbeam whilst the smokebox door has a rather crude 9H painted on. The engine had been allocated to the Lancashire depot since May 1964 but this image dates from the summer of 1967 just before withdrawal. *D.H.Beecroft*.

(*below*) Corkerhill Cl.5 No.73077 near Ribblehead on the Settle & Carlisle line with a fitted freight on 29th June 1963. This recent acquisition from Eastfield shed only had eighteen months life left but so much was happening as regards locomotive movements out of the ordinary nobody really noticed the rapidity with which steam was being withdrawn. *Paul Leavens*.

Creating a mini smoke-screen, St Rollox based Caprotti No.73147 departs from Perth with an Aberdeen-Glasgow express on 17th April 1965. The crew of resident Cl.4 tank No.80126 look on. *Paul Leavens*.

St Rollox Caprotti '5' No.73152, seen coupling up at Perth on 17th April 1965, was allocated to 65B for its whole eight and a half years existence. *Paul Leavens*.

(*above*) Heading for Glasgow with an express from Aberdeen, another of the St Rollox faithful No.73147 negotiates Hilton Junction on 15th April 1965. It seems strange that within a couple of months most of the 65B Cl.5s would be withdrawn. *Paul Leavens.*

(*below*) No.73111 KING UTHER at Nine Elms 30th March 1963. The locomotive was looking rather spruce but this may have been shortly after a visit to main works. The lack of a shedplate is unusual because No.73111 was a Nine Elms engine from new in October 1955 to August 1964 when it transferred to Eastleigh. *King of Britain. Father of Arthur by an adulterous amour with Igraine, widow of Gorlois, Duke of Cornwall, whom he later married. Uther was awarded the title Pendragon during the Saxon invasions of England in the late 5th Century. Gave the round table to Leodegrance who later gave the table to King Arthur as a dowry on the occasion of Arthur's marriage to Guinevere. Paul Leavens.*

Nine Elms based No.73088 JOYOUS GARD – another name in Arthurian legend for Alnwick Castle or Bamburgh Castle – rests at Salisbury shed circa 1962 along with various SR types and Cl.4 No.76017, a resident which would work its final days from this place. Note the ex-Great Western engines on the yard; their erstwhile shed located across on the Up side of the main line had closed in 1950 and since then the WR had kept a few engines at Salisbury SR for strategic purposes. Salisbury engine shed was in its final guise with a 'lightweight' roof provided by BR to replace – in 1955 – the front section of the more ornate L&SWR roof. Other SR sheds to get this BR style were Bournemouth, Bricklayers Arms, and Tunbridge Wells West for instance. *Paul Leavens*.

(*above*) Dusk at Weymouth on Saturday 11th February 1967 No.73080 along with Cl.4 No.76008 out in the cold whilst 'West Country' No.34040 CREWKERNE resides in the shed. No.73080 had been withdrawn in December whilst the 2-6-0 beneath the sheerlegs was still operational – on paper. Our '5' was another of the named engines and became MERLIN from 11th February 1961. Of course everyone knows *Merlin was a bard, soothsayer, and most famously an enchanter at King Arthur's court. He supplied the round table which seated 150 knights to Arthur's father Uther Pendragon, King of Britain. Paul Leavens.*

(*below*) No.73092 at Weymouth shed after the July 1967 surrender. Its final shed was Guildford where cleaners didn't exist as such, much like BR in general. The livery on this engine was lined green believe it or not. No.73092 was one of the engines swapped from Patricroft to Shrewsbury in August 1959 for one of the WR's Caprotti examples – 73090 to 73099 were involved north to south whilst Nos.73125 to 73134 went south to north. The Caprotti's all stayed put to withdrawal whereas the conventional valve gear engines were all over the WR and SR systems. Somewhat ironically three of them actually made it back to Patricroft in July 1965 for their 1967 withdrawals. *D.H.Beecroft.*

(*above*) Salisbury again but now with Nine Elms based No.73115 running between the shed and the coaling stage in August 1966. We have yet another Cl.5 which acquired an Arthurian name – KING PELLINORE – on 14th February 1960 but which has now lost the name. *The King was ruler of Listinoise (located, some say, in south-west Wales) and was the father of Sir Lamorack of Gales. Paul Leavens*.

(*below*) It looks as though Exmouth Junction's No.73162 is off to find Friary engine shed on the other side of Plymouth after working into the city on 5th August 1964. We are at Devonport (Kings Road) overlooking the throat at the eastern end of the passenger station from the bridge carrying Paradise Road over the railway. Just behind the signal box can be seen the retaining wall marking the path of the ascending incline from Stonehouse Pool. The station, which opened in 1876, was just thirty-three days away from closure. Oh! Doctor Beeching! *Paul Leavens*.

(*above*) This is – apparently – No.73113 – and we can vouch for this – on Bournemouth shed yard circa 1966. The external condition of Southern Region locomotives in their entirety was nothing short of atrocious. Cleaning might have 'gone by the board' but mechanically the engines were sound thanks to a somewhat dedicated army of fitters who battled away in some awful conditions with ancient appliances and a top management which couldn't care less! This Standard was named LYONNESSE on Boxing Day 1959 – before the 26th December became a bank holiday – but had obviously lost the nameplates by this time. *Lyonnesse in Arthurian legend was a rich area of farm land which stretched beyond Land's End towards the Scilly Isles and which was also Tristram's home: Now submerged.* No.73113's home at this time was Weymouth until January 1967 when it was withdrawn. *Paul Leavens.*

(*below*) No.73087 runs through Woking on 8th June 1966 with a Down express. *Paul Leavens.*

(*above*) No.73019 at Bath Green Park shed in 1961. Turned and ready for another working to Bournemouth, the Cl.5 is on its second stay at 82F having resided here from June 1958 to July 1960. This particular stay lasted from October 1960 to April 1962 when it moved on to Gloucester Barnwood. Having started on the LM Region at Nottingham in October 1951, it ended its existence on the LMR at Bolton where it was condemned in January 1967. *Paul Leavens*.

(*below*) More ghostly offerings from February 1967! This time we are at Basingstoke where Nos.73037 (Nine Elms), and 73020 (Weymouth) were captured outside the shed with Rebuilt 'WC' No.34095 BRENTOR. *Paul Leavens*.

Guildford shed on the night before with No.73093 and Cl.3 No.77014. Note the wooden painted numberplate on the Cl.3. *Paul Leavens.*

They were everywhere! Nine Elms 14th January 1967. The only identifiable engine is Cl.5 No.73029 which had started life at Blackpool in January 1952. Thereafter it really did some wandering going to Bristol, Carmarthen, Bristol, again, Swindon, Weymouth, Eastleigh, Guildford and finally Nine Elms in June 1966. Withdrawal came with the ending of steam motive power on the SR in July 1967. *Paul Leavens.*

(*above*) A half-decent looking No.73065 at Nine Elms on 14th January 1967! This Cl.5 came to the Southern in November 1962 from Canklow, its previous shed at Millhouses having closed its doors so Rotherham would have to do in the interim. Again this 4-6-0 saw the end on the SR in July. Note those pristine cab windows! *Paul Leavens*.

(*below*) No.73020 hurries through Clapham Junction station on Saturday 3rd December 1966. At the time this '5' was allocated to Weymouth shed but I doubt that was its destination on the day. Note the wooden false numberplate adorning the smokebox door. Another SR engine which worked to the end but at Guildford shed for the last three months. *Paul Leavens*.

(*top*) The Southern certainly worked their Standard Cl.5 fleet: No.73117 heads a Down express through Basingstoke on 31st July 1965. This '5' was another of the namers – VIVIEN – which had lost its plates early on it appears. *Vivien was the Chief Lady of the Lake.* (*centre*) No.73117 again! Also at Basingstoke on the same day but travelling in the Up direction with another express! Oxley based Stanier Cl.5 No.44856 makes its way to the shed for servicing. (*above*) No.73118 departs from Southampton (Central) for the west with an afternoon express on 17th July 1965. Although the engine has retained the lining around the cab side sheets and tender, the Arthurian theme nameplates – KING LEODEGRANCE – fitted on the last day of February 1960 have gone. *The monarch was King of Camelard identified by some as a part of Cornwall. He was father of Queen Guinevere, wife of King Arthur. All Paul Leavens.*

(*top*) Approaching Mount Pleasant crossing at Highbridge with a special working for enthusiasts – *SOUTHERN WANDERER* – on 28th March 1965, Eastleigh Cl.5 No.73022 appears smartly turned-out for a change. (*centre*) Nearing Clapham Junction at an unknown date, the 1 in 334 gradient does not seem to bother Nine Elms based No.73115. (*above*) No.73012 was allocated to Swindon shed from November 1956 to January 1964 which by Standard standards was a long time. Prior to reaching 82C, it started life on the LM Region at Holbeck in August 1951 then moved to Millhouses two years later and then, before it could drop its fire, it was transferred to Shrewsbury. 1964 proved to be a bad year for the engine when after transferring to Llanelly it moved to Barrow Road in Bristol during June but in November it was withdrawn. Also in the picture from circa 1963 was 'Hall' No.6917 OLDLANDS HALL, and Tyseley based 8F No.48475. *All Paul Leavens*.

5: CLASS 4 4-6-0s

General - The eighty locomotives of which this class consisted – 75000 to 75079 – were all built at Swindon between May 1951 and June 1957. The original intention was to build ninety engines with ten destined for the Eastern Region but that final lot as cancelled in late 1956 as the realisation of the 1955 Modernisation Plan started to register. The London Midland Region received the greatest number of engines with forty-five eventually being allocated. The WR had twenty in two lots of ten whilst the Southern had just fifteen – 75065-75079 – of which a third went to Dover whilst Exmouth Junction at the other extreme of the region had the balance with all being delivered between August 1955 and January 1956 at a rate of almost one a week which was fairly sharp for Swindon. The WR got the initial batch – 75000-75009 – with seven going to Shrewsbury, two to Swindon, 75000 and 75006, and No.75004 to Bristol's Bath Road shed in August. It was then the turn of the LM Region to receive Nos.75010-75019 with the first five going to Patricroft and the others to Southport. Then things started to change in that the sequences of numerical order and delivery dates appeared slightly confused when of course it wasn't because Swindon had everything under control. No.75020-75029 for the WR should have appeared next but instead Nos.75030-75049 went into traffic on the LMR between June and October 1953. Again the division used multiples of five with Bletchley having the first ten, Bedford the next five and then the final five to Accrington. Resuming with 75020, Swindon turned out the next ten at a much slower rate between November 1953 and May 1954; they were allocated to Oswestry (3), Canton (2), and the last five to Laira. Following on numerically but some three years after 75049 arrived, the LMR received 75050 to 75064 between November 1956 and June 1957. These engines were divided between six different depots with the East Midlands sheds receiving a batch for the first time. However, between the last two LMR batches Swindon had not been idle and during the period from August 1955 to January 1956 they had built and supplied the Southern Region with Nos.75065 to 75079. The SR engines differed from the rest in being coupled to the much heavier BR1B tender whereas the others had the BR2 or similar BR2A which weighed just over 42-tons against the 51-tons of the 1B with its larger water and coal capacities. Many of the Western engines remained within the region but quite a few migrated to the LMR as August 1968 approached. The LM examples basically stayed put whereas the SR batch which started out as the first five to Dover and the rest to Exmouth Junction ended their days with a dozen being withdrawn from Eastleigh, two at Templecombe and one which escaped to Stoke-on-Trent.

Just prior to its transfer to Bournemouth, Dover based No.75069 was photographed working a train of Continental vans near Folkestone during the summer of 1959. The last of the Dover batch, this 4-6-0 is now preserved on the Severn Valley Railway. *Paul Leavens.*

(*above*) Willesden's No.75030 hauling empty stock through Kensall Green, north London, on the afternoon of Tuesday 8th August 1961; this engine had quite a varied albeit short career just on the LM Region. Besides working on the southern end of the WCML, the Class 4 also found employment in North Wales, briefly on the CLC, in the Potteries and finally banking on Shap for much of 1967. *Paul Leavens*.

(*below*) Another of the London Midland contingent – 75031 – works empty stock for Euston through Kensall Green at a later date, 17th March 1962. The engine at the time was on Willesden's strength and spent most of its time at 1A performing this type of work. By the end of the year it had moved to Aston. Note the BR2 tender which had a capacity of 3500 gallons of water and six tons of coal; it was of course equipped with a water scoop. *Paul Leavens*.

(*above*) A dramatic view of No.75070 crossing the viaduct at Redlesdown with a passenger train on Monday 2nd October 1961; the Cl.4 was allocated to Three Bridges depot at the time. *Paul Leavens*.

(*below*) Wearing the all-too-familiar coat of filth, No.75074 was stabled at Eastleigh shed in August 1956. This engine was barely ten months old but it's managed to accumulate such a mess. At least it survived to the end on the Southern, and at Eastleigh on its third residency there. *Paul Leavens*.

(*above*) No.75065 and cousin No.76063 rub shoulders with the enemy – BRC&W Type 3 diesel-electric D6548 – at Basingstoke shed on 17th July 1965. Basingstoke had by now lost its shed code 70D having been downgraded to a stabling point from September 1963. Nos.75065 and 75066 were both allocated to 70D until March 1963 when they were transferred to Eastleigh, at least on paper. *Paul Leavens*.

(*below*) Another former Basingstoke charge – No.75077 – which transferred to Nine Elms in March 1963 departs for the Capital with a bit of a mixed bag on 3rd April 1965, shortly before it was transferred to Eastleigh. Basingstoke shed had Nos.75075 to 75079 allocated from June 1956 until its 'down grade' and No.75074 from August 1957 to January 1959. Most of them later worked from Eastleigh to July 1967, and two of them are preserved! *Paul Leavens*.

No.75069 again, this time one of Eastleigh's, its final shed. With twelve on, the Cl.4 shows off at Deepcut on 3rd July 1965. *Paul Leavens*.

No.75022 shows off the mixed traffic capabilities of the class when working a goods train through Oxford on 16th March 1963. *Paul Leavens*.

No.75022 again, but now at Plymouth's former SR station at Friary on 7th November 1964! *Paul Leavens*.

No.75019 at Eastleigh 2nd October 1965 when it was a Skipton engine; this engine ended up at Carnforth and worked right through to that fateful month of August 1968. *Paul Leavens*.

No.75070 showing off the capabilities of this class again whilst working an RCTS special between Dean and East Grinstead on the Salisbury-Southampton line on 20th March 1966. *Paul Leavens.*

One time resident No.75077 but now allocated to Eastleigh shares one of the Nine Elms stables with two other visitors, MN No.35030 ELDER DEMPSTER LINES from Weymouth, and complete stranger A4 No.60024 KINGFISHER from Aberdeen Ferryhill. The Scottish Region engine must have been taking part in a rail tour otherwise it would have been employed on the 3-hour expresses between Aberdeen and Glasgow. The date of this nocturnal image is 20th March 1966, a Sunday but we are not sure if it was an early morning or late evening exposure? *Paul Leavens.*

(*above*) Front end comparisons can now be made: No.75079 on the left with 76057 on the right at Eastleigh motive power depot 11th February 1967. Considering the works at Eastleigh was not involved in the production of any of the Standard locomotives, it certainly took care of a number of them when they were operational. *Paul Leavens*.

No.75075 hauling an Up working of military hardware at Worting Junction 7th April 1966. *Paul Leavens*.

Shortly before the shut-down, Nos.75027 and 75019 await instructions at Carnforth in July 1968! They had both come from Tebay in January and had basically followed each other from their short meeting at Skipton in November 1966. No.75019 had spent its whole short life on the LMR whereas 75027 began its career on the WR at Laira before joining the LMR in 1965 but it basically spent the latter half of 1965, nearly all of 1966, and all of 1967 in store. No.75019 took part in virtually the same sleepathon! *Paul Leavens*.

With its exhaust hiding the twisted spire in the background, Nottingham Cl.4 No.75063 heads north out of Chesterfield with a working to Sheffield in 1961. *SVMRC*.

(*above*) Running over the junction at Peterborough East which will enable the Cl.4 and its train to gain some height and run through Nene Junction and then join the ECML at Crescent Junction for the Peterborough (North) stop, Leicester Midland's No.75040 works west in July 1960 with a service from Peterborough (East) to Leicester. *SVMRC.*

(*below*) No.75003 from Tyseley negotiates the junctions at Hatton Bank whilst working a Down mineral train on an unknown date in 1961. One of the original WR allocation this engine remained on the region to withdrawal from Worcester in October 1965. *SVMRC.*

6: CLASS 4 2-6-0s

General – Every region but the Western received some of these Class 4MT 2-6-0s with the Southern taking the lion's share, just! The Scottish Region saw the first examples released to traffic with five arriving at Motherwell from Horwich during December 1952. At the same time Doncaster was turning out Nos.76020-76024 for the North Eastern and this group of five all went to different sheds with Darlington, York, Dairycoates, Sunderland, and Gateshead getting one each as a taster! There was then a lull from Doncaster until October 1953 when over the next two months they put out ten into traffic with five for the SR and five for the Eastern Region – 76030-76034. Over the summer of 1954 Doncaster produced another ten engines for the ER – 76035-76044 – which completed that region's allocation. After that lot things began to get untidy regarding delivery dates and engine numbers with Doncaster then putting three for the North Eastern into traffic – 76050-76052 – during August and September 1956 whilst during the same period July and August 1956 they sent Nos.76063-76069 off to the Southern. Taking a step back into 1955 and we find Doncaster has produced Nos.76045-76049 in March and April for the NER and then followed that lot with 76053-76062 for the SR. Now, numerically we are getting straight again with Nos.76070-76074 – for the ScR – coming out of Doncaster during the period September to November 1956. Then Horwich starts-up again and over the twelve months from December 1956 to November 1957 they built some twenty-five Cl.4s – 76075-76099 – for the LMR and ScR with ten going to the latter region. During 1957 the Scottish Region was the recipient of another fifteen – 76100-76114 – engines, all from Doncaster and all of them spread around various sheds. Many of these engines remained with their parent regions although the Eastern gave theirs up to the SR and LMR during 1962.

Resident No.76105 at Bathgate shed in 1965. *Chris Dunne.*

(*above*) Grangemouth was another Scottish depot which offered lodgings for the Cl.4s and here in 1963 an atrocious looking No.76113 stables outside the shed with the water bag just on the lip of the filler cap as per 'It's Saturday afternoon and everyone has disappeared!' Note the three-link coupling adjacent to the screw coupling used for ease when working with unfitted goods wagons. From here this engine moved to Carstairs in October 1965 and a year later it was withdrawn. *D.H.Beecroft*.

(*below*) No.76109 was delivered new to Thornton Junction shed in August 1957 – along with 76110 and 76111 – but in January 1960 it transferred to Dunfermline – followed in April by 76110 and 76111 – where further employment in the coal moving business was assured. Here at Alloa sub-shed on a Saturday afternoon in 1963 the 2-6-0 settles in for the weekend sandwiched between unidentified J38s. *D.H.Beecroft*.

Southern Region – The SR received the first of their allocation – 76005 to 76019 – when No.76005 arrived at Eastleigh shed just prior to Christmas 1952. Over the next eight months the fifteen 2-6-0s were released from Horwich at the rate of two a month and all of them were initially shedded at Eastleigh. However, by the middle of the following summer a couple of them had transferred to Bournemouth whilst others went later to Brighton, Guildford, Redhill, Salisbury and Yeovil Town. In October 1953 a further batch – 76025 to 76029 – started to arrive from Doncaster shops and all of these went to Eastleigh shed too. It was April 1955 before the SR received any more of these Class 4s when Doncaster sent Nos.76053 to 76062 to Redhill shed. That batch had all been delivered by July; following on were Nos.76063 to 76069, which all reverted to the Eastleigh venue but not until a year to the day after 76062 had gone to Redhill. At least four of the 1956 lot remained allocated to 71A and were withdrawn from that shed during 1965 and 1967. That proved to be the last of the new engines sent to the SR but in November 1962 five more of the class – 76030 to 76034 – were allocated to the Southern from the Eastern and these went to Brighton until September 1963 when Guildford acquired all five of them. So, that was the SR allocation sorted out but another shed saw their services in 1965 when Feltham in south-west London received Nos.76053, 76055 and 76066 for six months.

Class 4 2-6-0 No.76010 had two stints allocated to Eastleigh shed, the first when new from March 1952 to September 1958, and the second residency from January 1959 after a four-month transfer to Yeovil. The second 'go' mimicked sister No.76011 which also left 71A in October 1965 for Bournemouth. However, 76010 was withdrawn from Bournemouth in September 1966 whereas 76011 remained active until July 1967 when all Southern Region steam was condemned. This image was undated but would have been around 1960. Note the wrong facing BR crest on the tender. *K.R.Pirt.*

(*above*) No.76015 went new to Eastleigh in May 1953 then in June 1961 it transferred to Bournemouth. It belonged to the latter shed when this undated view was captured at Bournemouth (Central) from where it was working a morning passenger train. It was one of the early casualties of the steam cull being condemned in October 1965. *SVMRC*.

(*below*) An undated image of No.76009 at Weymouth shed towards or just after the end. Bournemouth was its final shed and many of that depot's charges were taken away to Weymouth for storage pending sale. *D.H.Beecroft*.

(*above*) An externally smart looking No.76067 gets attention from its crew on 2nd October 1965. The seventeen engines built for the Southern at Doncaster in 1955 and 1956 all had the larger BR1B flush-sided tenders which weighed almost ten tons more than the BR2 and BR2A coupled to the rest of the class. No.76067 had been a Salisbury resident since March 1960 and would be transferred to Bournemouth in April 1967. *Paul Leavens*.

(*below*) Eastleigh's No.76066 shows off its tender to good advantage at Nine Elms shed on 9th October 1965. Behind these 2-6-0s, the tenders did look rather large though. *Paul Leavens*.

7: CLASS 3 2-6-0

North Eastern – Swindon managed to complete the building of all twenty of the BR Standard Class 3MT 2-6-0s they were entrusted to construct during 1954. The score of locomotives were split 50-50 between the North Eastern and Scottish regions on the basis of 5, 5, 5, and 5 as put into traffic. Darlington shed was the recipient of the NE Region lot with Nos.77000 to 77003 all recorded as arriving in February 1954 and 77004 in March. In the following June No.77010 turned up along with Nos.77011 and 77012; Nos.77013 and 77014 arrived in July. All ten engines seemingly moved about the region with impunity and some engines managed up to fifteen transfers during their short lives. Eight of the NE batch were condemned on the region but two stole away to the LMR at Northwich in November 1964 and then one of those went even further ending its days at Guildford where it managed to scratch a living from March 1966 to July 1967. None of the class was preserved and all went to private scrap yards located in Derbyshire (2), Lancashire (1), Scotland (10), Wales (1), and Yorkshire (6). **Scottish Region** – The ScR received their first example of the BR Standard Class 3MT 2-6-0 at Dawsholm in March 1954 when No.77005 was allocated for what must have been one of the shortest stints anywhere; the Cl.3 departed for Hamilton later that month and no other Cl.3 was ever shedded at Dawsholm again. Nos.77006 and 77007 went direct from the makers to Hamilton shed in March and April respectively whilst sisters 77008 and 77009 went to Perth in April and June 1954 also respectively; these latter pair actually went to Perth's sub at Blair Atholl for banking duties but during the winter of that first year had transferred to Polmadie. What the reason was for the delivery delay with 77009 is unknown but shortage of materials during those late post-war years was still problematic. The Regions' next batch – Nos.77015 to 77019 – proved to be not only the last Scottish examples but also the last BR engines from this class. That clutch of five 2-6-0s was delivered during the summer months of 1954. They all went to Hurlford on the former Glasgow & South Western line and were employed on mine runs besides working local passenger and pick-up freights. No.77007 joined them at Hurlford in August 1963 and all six of were withdrawn at various dates during 1966 as were the other four which had migrated to Motherwell in two lots from the summer of 1963 – 77005 and 77008 – and Nos.77006 and 77009 in October 1965.

It was new once! This is No.77003 on 14th June 1954 just four months after leaving Swindon shops in a pristine condition – WD No.90424 poking out of the shed behind was ex-works 10th June 1954 after a Heavy General overhaul! During the following July No.77003 was transferred to West Auckland along with the rest of that first Darlington based batch. All but two of the ten NE Region engines were sent to West Auckland during that first year of operation on the region. *Paul Leavens.*

Two together in York shed on Saturday 8th October 1966. Nos.77012 and 77002 were both still operational and allocated here although 77002 has lost its works plate, smokebox numberplate and shed plate – it has probably just arrived from Stourton its last posting where all five of the first NE Region batch were allocated circa 1963/64 – but is remarkably clean for the period. No.77012 has both number and shed plates but the latter is a 50D Goole plate and since it left there in March 1966 it was supposed to transfer to South Blyth but that move didn't materialise and a transfer to York in April was undertaken instead; why the plate was still in situ is a mystery but it was better than nothing if a little confusing. Both of these engines were condemned in June 1967 and sold to a scrap yard in Chesterfield the following year. *Paul Leavens*.

No.77014 one of two that escaped – with 77011 – from the NE Region to the LM Region at Northwich in November 1964. But then No.77014 took another great stride and ended up on the Southern at Guildford in March 1966. Being a one-off even from a small class, the engine was in demand for rail tours and such like and on 16th October 1966 it was one of the star attractions heading various sections of the Locomotive Club of Great Britain's Dorset and Hants Rail Tour. Here the Class 3 has the whole train at Ringwood. Although 70C did not exactly 'go to town' cleaning their charge, it looks reasonable compared with some of the SR Pacifics especially. This engine was the last operational member of the class and was withdrawn in July 1967 as steam on the Southern was brought to its finale! *Paul Leavens*.

(*above*) No.77007 completed and ready for running-in at Swindon on 28th March 1954. These engines were sent on goods trains as far as Plymouth on occasion but their main trials area was over the M&SWJR besides locals to Bristol. How long it actually took them to make the 400-odd mile run to their new Scottish homes is unknown but if the WCML sheds were anything like the ECML sheds were with ex-Doncaster deliveries, the period could be somewhat protracted. *Paul Leavens*.

(*below*) No.77019 working at Crewe in September 1954 whilst en route from Swindon to Hurlford; how long Crewe held onto the 2-6-0 is unknown but some reports suggest that being the last of the class, it was being evaluated! *Paul Leavens*.

(*above*) No.77018 on a local passenger working at Newton-on-Ayr on 7th April 1966. *Paul Leavens*.

(*below*) By now Motherwell based, No.77005 has charge of an enthusiasts' brake van special at Holytown on 8th April 1966 on the line from Wishaw to Bellshill. The station here was opened by the Caledonian Railway in June 1880 as Carfin, which became Carfin Junction in 1882. It was renamed Holytown Junction later that year then, from 1901, simply Holytown; it is still open. Note the coal train being aided by a pair of Clayton Type 1 diesels. Just six months away from withdrawal, the Cl.3 was sold to a local though very large scrap metal concern at nearby Wishaw. *Paul Leavens*.

8: CLASS 2MT 2-6-0

Western Region – Darlington was responsible for building all sixty-five of these Class 2MT 2-6-0s and the Western Region was the first to benefit from their delivery during the period December 1952 to April 1953. All ten went to Oswestry though three of them spent a couple of months in Swindon store prior to delivery to 89A. After that initial burst the building of further examples ceased until later in the year when Darlington started on a batch of thirty-five locomotives. **North Eastern Region** – The NER started to receive the early examples of their assigned batch of ten Class 2 tender engines – 78010 to 78019 – from Darlington in time for Christmas 1953. West Auckland shed took in the first nine with delivery complete by March 1954. The tenth and final engine was allocated to Kirkby Stephen, also in March, with some of the West Auckland lot – 78016 to 78018 – following it to 51H in April. No.78013 also went to Kirkby Stephen in January 1958 until June 1960 when it left the NE Region for another Kirkby on the LM Region. 78013 was however not the first of the Cl.2s to depart to the LMR as Nos.78017 and 78019 had left for Wigan in April whilst 78018 has gone to Chester at the same time. Other members of the NER batch moved away in 1963 and 1964 with Polmadie, Gorton, and Motherwell all receiving one or more. Only one engine never left the North Eastern and that was No.78015 which was still allocated to Darlington shed when it was condemned in November 1963 – the first of the class – and was then cut up at Darlington its birthplace in January 1964. For the record it is worth mentioning that two of the NE Region engines – 78018 and 78019 – have been preserved. **London Midland Region** – Following on from the NER order, Nos.78020-78044 started to emerge from Darlington at a rate of approximately three a month from April to December 1954. No less than ten different sheds on the LMR were to receive one or more of these useful 2-6-0s. The next batch for the LM – Nos.78055 to 78064 – began delivery from August to November 1956. These were destined for just two sheds – Chester Northgate and Wigan Central – with each having five engines. After those initial allocations the LM engines transferred all over the region but none went to the ER or SR which essentially never saw the class. **Scottish Region** – The ScR managed to be the recipients of ten Class 2s – 78045 to 78054 – with the first of them going to Kittybrewster in October 1955. Hawick got the next two with a pair also going to Edinburgh's St Margarets. Motherwell took the last five during November and December 1955. Darlington was turning these 2-6-0s out in batches of ten alphabetically but not one after the other. Instead there was a gap between batches as materials were gathered. Between No.78044 which went to the LM Region and 78045 there was a gap of ten months. Likewise from the delivery of 78054 to Motherwell and the entry to traffic on the LM Region of No.78055 was a gap of eight months. Darlington was of course building other locomotives and the ubiquitous BR 350 h.p. 0-6-0DE shunter was at the forefront of the manufacturing effort. Meanwhile, all of the ScR Standard 2s remained on the region throughout their lives with many other sheds having the use of their services including: Aberdeen Ferryhill; Aviemore; Ayr; Bathgate; Dawsholm; Dumfries; Helmsdale; Inverness; Keith; Perth; and Stirling. Besides the ten designated engines odd examples arrived in Scotland from other regions: 78026 arrived from Canklow in January 1962 and added Corkerhill and Stranraer to the list of sheds served by the class. In March 1963 No.78010 was transferred to Polmadie for a couple months until moving to Motherwell in May and then retiring back to the England in June. Also in 1963 No.78016 came to Motherwell in August, it was withdrawn from Stranraer in August 1966. November 1966 saw the last of the Cl.2s in Scotland, their withdrawals starting in July 1964 when Nos.78048 from Hawick and 78053 from Stirling were condemned.

No.78028 shunts at Leicester's West Bridge goods yard on 17th July 1964. Allocated at the time to Coalville shed, the 2MT spent much of its life working from Leicester Midland shed but this duty entailed a Coalville engine working the branch on a daily trip with freight for West Bridge. The route saw trains negotiating Glenfield tunnel which had clearance restrictions and required the BR Standard Cl.2 to have the cab roof modified for running through the one-mile long bore. Note the legend 15E painted in place of a shed plate on the smokebox door. No.78013 was similarly modified for the Leicester West Bridge freights. *David Dalton.*

78026 awaits running-in trials at Darlington shed on 6th June 1954 prior to delivery to Canklow, the first of two allocated to the shed. B16/1 No.61432 from Neville Hill shed has just completed a Heavy General overhaul and is also ready for road tests. Both locomotives were built at Darlington but some thirty-three years apart. After the Cl.2s eight years at Canklow, it transferred to Ayr and thereafter finished its life working from ScR sheds. *Paul Leavens.*

(*below*) The most northerly allocated BR Standard on record! No.78052 held that record for eighteen months and in fact still holds the mantle because it will never now be broken. Our subject is seen running round at Dornoch terminus on Tuesday 5th August 1958 when it was standing in for the usual ex-WR Pannier No.1646 which was then the branch engine. The 60C shed plate denotes Helmsdale which from February 1957 to September 1958 was home for the Cl.2 which took turns in running the Dornoch branch from The Mound or stood down as stand-by engine whilst the 0-6-0PT got on with the work. The story of the Dornoch branch motive power situation is quite well known but in a nutshell ex-Highland Railway 0-4-4T No.55053 – the last of her kind – was overcome by old-age in February 1957 and a replacement had to be found – quickly! The nature of the branch demanded a 'lightweight' locomotive and so the only suitable type was a Western Region Pannier tank but it would be April before one could be delivered to the far-north line. Step in BR Std. Cl.2 No.78052 which was working from Inverness shed at the time and was but a few hours away. The Cl.2 worked the branch until No.1646 arrived but was afterwards kept on as 'spare' for the time being, in case! During 1958 a decision was taken to bring in another Pannier and so No.1649 came from Bristol in August enabling No.78052 to return to more taxing duties. For the record the Cl.2 went to St Margarets from here; two months later to Aviemore in November; Perth in July 1962; finally Bathgate in November 1963 where it worked until January 1966. *David Dalton.*

(*top*) No.78052 at the north end of the branch – The Mound – on that Tuesday in August 1958! *David Dalton*. (*centre*) No.78045 on the branch to St Combs without a cow-catcher on 28th March 1964! *David Dalton*. (*below*) No.78051 during its sojourn at Dumfries shed from July 1964 to June 1966 when it moved to Ayr shed; this image was dated 6th April 1966. *Paul Leavens*.

9: CLASS 4MT 2-6-4T

Scottish Region – The ScR was not the first region to receive the Standard Class 4 2-6-4T although numerically Nos.80000 to 80009 were earmarked to be supplied by Derby between September 1952 and January 1953 and to be allocated to Ayr (1), Corkerhill (2), Kittybrewster (2), Motherwell (2) and Polmadie (3); all sheds which would later be recipients of larger numbers of the mixed traffic tanks and some of which already had engines from the initial order – 80020 to 80030 – supplied by Brighton. As it turned out the design was basically superb and there was nothing which was beyond the capabilities of the engines. Having been operational on other regions since July 1951 the prowess of the 2-6-4T was already appreciated by the time the initial eleven for the Scottish lines were being delivered. No less than twenty-five engine sheds in Scotland housed one or more of the Class 4 tank and besides those already mentioned the following were also involved: Ardrossan, Beattock, Carstairs, Dalry Road, Dawsholm, Dumfries, Dundee, Dundee (Tay Bridge), Eastfield, Ferryhill, Greenock (Ladyburn), Hamilton, Hawick, Hurlford, Keith, Perth, Stirling, St Margarets, Stranraer, and St Rollox. Nos.80020 to 80030 were in fact the first members of the class allocated to Scottish sheds and these were delivered from Brighton between October 1951 to February 1952 with Kittybrewster, Polmadie, Corkerhill and Ayr sharing the spoils. 80054 to 80058 were the next lot numerically to arrive – ex Derby – and all five were sent to Polmadie around Christmas 1954. Preceding them from October 1954 was Nos.80106 to 80115 from Brighton shared between Kittybrewster and Polmadie. Yet another batch came in July 1955 – 80121 to 80130 – which were spread around amongst Dundee, Kittybrewster, Perth, Polmadie, and Stirling. That ended the arrival of the new examples but further engines were cascaded from other regions over the ensuing years giving Scotland an embarrassment of riches to the point where locomotives were being withdrawn simply because they were surplus but were barely ten years old. Many returned south to England re-instated after withdrawal in Scotland.
Southern Region – Nos.80010 to 80019 arrived on the SR between July and October 1951, ten engines all allocated to Tunbridge Wells West. That then was it until 1956 as regards new engines when Nos.80145 to 80154 were sent new to Brighton shed from Brighton works between October 1956 and March 1957. All the new engines in the interim had gone to the LMR (45), ER (36), NER (8), ScR (36). In 1959 somebody in one of the motive power departments had a brainwave whereby it was decided that all the Fairburn LMS Cl.4 2-6-4 tanks working on the Southern which had been built at Brighton should be swapped with the BR Standard Cl.4 tanks working on the LMR. The numbers involved were about equal so no one region would go short. So, in December 1959 the deed was undertaken and completed without a hitch; the age of the engines involved was also roughly the same.

No.80092 is highlighted by the morning sun at Perth shed in circa 1963. Rubbing shoulders with Gresley A4s, the six-coupled tank found employment on the Killin branch for instance. No.80092 started life at Kentish Town on the LMR but came to Scotland and 63A in March 1960 to add to the already growing numbers of the class north of the border. In the background stands the LMS-built enginemen's barracks which overlooked the shed yard as if to remind the footplate crews why they were really there! *K.R.Pirt, Book Law collection.*

No.80012 in amongst the big boys at Nine Elms on 14th January 1967; after a lifetime working from Southern Region sheds, No.80012 finished off at Nine Elms, arriving in October 1965 from Eastleigh. It managed seven sheds in fourteen years with long stays and short stays. Stewarts Lane was the shortest at six months whilst Tunbridge Wells West was easily the longest residency at six years and eight months! Withdrawn 19th March 1967, this Cl.4 tank was sold to a scrap yard in South Wales. *Paul Leavens.*

An all stations Redhill-Reading service runs into platform 2 at Crowthorne on the morning of 3rd January 1965 with Redhill based No.80151 in charge. This Cl.4 was another engine which had remained on the SR throughout its life. Note the lack of a 75B shedplate. In June 80151 would venture west to Salisbury but would spend much of its time in store but in October 1966 Eastleigh beckoned with six months of work before it all ended. However, by some good fortune 80151 was sold for scrap to a yard in South Wales and today the Cl.4 is thriving in preservation. *Paul Leavens.*

(*above*) Eastleigh based No.80139 departs from Southampton (Central) with an Up service on the morning of 10th July 1965. This was another of the Cl.4 tanks swapped in December 1959 having started life at Neasden with 80137 to 80144 during the early summer of 1956. *Paul Leavens*.

(*below*) No.80102 at Basingstoke shed on 17th July 1965 with 'West Country' No.34001 EXETER and another Standard for company on a pleasant summer evening. This Cl.4 had started out on the Eastern Region at Plaistow in March 1955; in July 1962 it went to the WR at Old Oak Common but then was called to the LMR at Shrewsbury. In April 1965 with no work to give the tank, No.80102 was sent to the SR at Eastleigh and in December it was condemned only to be cut-up in a local goods yard the following year. *Paul Leavens*.

No.80035 on Watford shed yard in 1958 wearing a wrong-facing BR crest received at an unrecorded overhaul during the previous twelve months. This engine was destined originally for the Southern along with 80034 to 80039 but instead that batch was diverted to the LMR with 80034 to 80038 being allocated to Watford. However, in order to straighten the books, they were all transferred to the SR at Ashford in December 1959; a batch of LMS-derived Cl.4 tanks based at SR sheds were being swapped for these and other Standard Cl.4s. *Paul Leavens*.

(*above*) A solitary No.80143 in the yard at Nine Elms on 1st January 1966; withdrawal was some eighteen months away on that last day but the Cl.4 looks as though it has already thrown-in-the-towel! No doubt somebody would come along with a shovelful of embers and revitalise No.80143 before much longer. *Paul Leavens*.

(*below*) One of Brighton's Cl.4s – 80153 – working hard through Selsdon with a London Bridge-Brighton service in 1960! *Paul Leavens*.

(above) A pre-December 1959 image of Watford's No.80034 at the southern end of its territory working in and around Euston carriage sidings in between trips along the WCML to Watford and beyond! *SVMRC*.

(below) No.80145 alongside platform 17 at Clapham Junction station on 19th October 1966! *Paul Leavens*.

10: CLASS 3 2-6-2T

General – Swindon was responsible for building the whole of the forty-five engines in this class, the main reason being the adoption of the Swindon No.4 boiler as there was no equivalent type of boiler in the BR Standard designs. The boiler had to be adapted to fit the locomotives – the Class 3 77XXX class also received these adapted Swindon No.4 boilers hence their origins – but it was a proven piece of hardware used by the ex-GWR 41XX and 56XX classes for instance. The Southern allocation consisted Nos.82010 to 82019 and these came out from Swindon between June and September 1952 being shedded initially at Exmouth Junction (was there a prophecy by Swindon that they would eventually take over this shed and a large chunk of the SR territory in Devon and Cornwall?). In late 1954 72A received another new batch – 82022 to 82025 – which all remained at the depot until transferred to Eastleigh in September 1962 which in turn was short-lived because they were moved on to Nine Elms two months later. What of the other ten? They too did the Eastleigh then Nine Elms shuffle but at different times with three of them transferring to 71A in 1952 and one in 1953. Nos.82015 and 82016 arrived at Nine Elms in March 1963 via three months at Guildford whereas the rest had moved to London during November and December 1962. Of the locomotives sent new to either the North Eastern or Western regions, seven of them ended their days at Nine Elms (a number worked from Exmouth Junction shed too but 72A was part of the WR by then) too bringing 70A's allocation to twenty-one.

No.82016 was one of those which transferred during the early days from Exmouth Junction to Eastleigh making the move with sister 82015 in October 1952. The same pair did that little wobble towards Guildford shed between December 1962 and March 1963. Recorded in this image at Eastleigh shed on 30th July 1954, the 2-6-2T was used for empty carriage duties at Southampton and for working freights on the Fawley branch either solo or in conjunction with its sister when heavy oil trains were encountered. *K.R.Pirt, Book Law collection.*

New No.82031 undergoing a steam test at Swindon prior to being released to traffic at Barry in December 1954! *Paul Leavens*.

A glorious Sunday morning on 12th March 1967 sees No.82019 bathed in sunlight and being prepared by its crew prior to a day on e.c.s. jobs to and from Waterloo. This engine had spent its first ten years working around Devon along with sisters 82010 to 82018 but in September 1962 as the WR took over everything west of Salisbury those ten Cl.3 tanks transferred to Eastleigh as a stop-gap for a few weeks before reporting en masse to the Foreman at Nine Elms where they all worked to withdrawal. Nos.82022 to 82025 which had also been at 72A from new joined them on the migration to London. Our subject engine was the only one of the batch to work until the final day. But others came to Nine Elms during 1964 and 1965: Nos.82026-82029 came from Bournemouth in September 1964 followed by 82005, 82006, 82020 and 82021 from Machynlleth and 82033 from Bangor in April 1965. Only 82029 of that batch survived to 9th July 1967. *Paul Leavens*.

(*above*) No.82037 takes water at Wells (Tucker Street) after completing a run from Bristol on 8th June 1963. Three months hence the line from Bristol to Witham and all the stations thereon, including Wells, would be closed as per the instructions of one Dr Beeching! *Paul Leavens*.

(*below*) Bristol Barrow Road shed had a number of the Cl.3s from about September 1960 and this was the kind of duty entrusted to them: No.82035 departs from Wookey on 8th June 1963 on a Bristol-Wells service. At the finish of the summer timetable No.82035 would be put into storage until the end of the year. Wookey station was closed as and from 9th September 1963 along with all the stations on the line from Bristol to Witham; another piece of British railway history was thus completed! *Paul Leavens*.

(*above*) Green Park shed in Bath had six of these engines allocated at various times and some, including No.82004 illustrated here, were withdrawn at this depot. The Cl.3 came from the Western Region and Wellington (84H) in particular during October 1959. *Paul Leavens*.

(*below*) Just over a year later No.82041 was captured on film at 82E. This engine had arrived in Bath slightly earlier in March 1959 and it too was condemned here. *Paul Leavens*.

No.82022 in the vast yard with served Nine Elms engine shed. With hindsight it seems extraordinary that the sheds here and the facilities were all accessed via one turntable which had something of a remarkable existence being rarely out of commission! *Paul Leavens.*

These images of various members of the class at Nine Elms engine shed are illustrating the numerous shades of dirt and levels of contamination displayed by these locomotives. *Pail Leavens.*

(*above*) No.82027 still working on New Year's Day 1966; this Cl.3 had started life on the North Eastern Region at Kirkby Stephen in November 1954 and had been to virtually all corners of that region prior to transferring to the SR and Guildford in September 1963. Arriving at Nine Elms in September 1964, it was at this depot where No.82027 was condemned just eight days after this image was recorded. *Paul Leavens*.

(*below*) Apparently No.82006 was in green livery but without lining when it was photographed in the shed yard at 70A on 5th March 1966. This was another ex-WR engine which was amongst the first ten of the class which were allocated new to Tyseley shed between April and June 1952. *Paul Leavens*.

Our old friend No.82019 meets opposition at Clapham Junction on 26th November 1966. *Paul Leavens.*

No.82014 takes on water at Eastleigh in May 1961. *Paul Leavens.*

18th September 1966 at Nine Elms and decay was beginning to take hold. No.82006 had been here since April 1965 courtesy of the Western Region's Welsh branch and had already lost its smokebox number plate. It had actually succumbed to withdrawal on this very day. It was sold in December and taken away to South Wales. The removal of one of the front protection plates enables us to see the lubricator and the lubrication lines leading to. Behind is Cl.4 No.80012 which remained operational until the following summer. Beyond 'BB' No.34057 BIGGIN HILL is in steam and ready for another job. *Paul Leavens*.

(*above*) No.82006 freshly out-shopped at Swindon circa August 1957 in lined green livery with the newly introduced – but in this instance on this side – wrong facing BR crest. The engine was part of the Wellington (84H) allocation at this period along with sisters 82004 and 82009. *K.R.Pirt, Book Law Publications*.

(*below*) No.82043 at its home shed Barry on 12th August 1956. This Cl.3 had arrived here new in June 1955 and had followed 82035, 82036, a belated 82037, 82039 to 82042; No.82044 the last of the class had followed them all arriving in August. Nos.82030 to 82032 has been the advance party during Christmas 1954 but had moved on shortly afterwards. All of those from the 1955 intake moved away during the late spring and early summer of 1958 as diesel multiple units took over the local passenger services. No.82043 went to Bristol and up to its February 1964 withdrawal worked from all three of the motive power depots there. Three weeks at Taunton in early 1962 doesn't really count! *David Dalton*.

11: CLASS 2MT 2-6-2T

General – The BR Standard Class 2MT 2-6-2T was a virtual copy of Ivatt's LMS Cl.2MT 2-6-2 tank engine with a few minor design changes and modifications which were easily discernible. All were built at Crewe, the works responsible for building most of the Ivatt engines and the first examples appeared in the summer of 1953 with Nos.84000 to 84004 going to the London Midland Region at Plodder Lane shed in Bolton during August and September. Their duties there included haulage of the Bolton (Great Moor Street) to Manchester (Exchange) local passenger services via Worsley and Eccles over the former L&NWR lines. The next fifteen engines also went to LM Region sheds with Bedford, Burton, Bury, Low Moor, and Royston – the last two sheds were still LMR property then – all receiving varying numbers. The final ten – 84020 to 84029 – all went to the Southern Region with Ashford and Ramsgate sharing the spoils equally. Whilst resident on the SR the Cl.2s did not remain at their initial allocated sheds and instead moved around to all corners of the region to the following depots at various times: Bricklayers Arms, Brighton, Eastleigh, Exmouth Junction, and Stewarts Lane but by September 1961 they had been gathered together and sent to the LMR where it was becoming difficult to find suitable work for their own twenty engines without having another ten thrown into the mix. Storage beckoned for many of the class and many of them found little or no work; the advent of the diesel multiple units combined with closures of branch lines and stations saw these push-pull fitted locomotives losing work virtually every week. The first withdrawal took place on 12th October 1963 when No.84012 of Southport shed was condemned at Crewe and cut up almost immediately. Thereafter some nine withdrawals took place in 1964 whilst 1965 saw the class become extinct, the last ten all being withdrawn together in December 1965. A final word on the proposed but eventually abandoned scheme to modify ten of the class for work on the Isle-of-Wight to replace the O2 tank engines; the engines were apparently gathered at Eastleigh for the work to begin on the modifications but a last minute hitch saw the plan discarded and the 2-6-2Ts returned from whence they came. It was that bunch of ten which became the last of the class.

Ex-works at Crewe North shed in October 1963 whilst allocated to 15B Wellingborough shed. Note that the engine has had a partial repaint on specific areas indicating an Intermediate overhaul but at this time many of the class were in store or withdrawn awaiting sale. Any repair would appear to be a bonus but at ten years old No.84008 could be condemned at any time and indeed that did eventually happen on 30th October 1965. None of the class survived and as we go to press one preservation group is happily building a new BR Standard Class 2MT 2-6-2T which will be numbered 84030! *Chris Dunne.*

(*above*) No.84003 resident at Wrexham Rhossdu in 1955; this was the engine's second allocation having departed Plodder Lane in March 1954. Except for a five-year stint at Birkenhead from July 1956, No.84003 spent the rest of its life working from sheds in North Wales: Rhyl, Llandudno Junction, Croes Newydd, Llandudno Junction in that order. It was withdrawn 2nd October 1965 at the latter shed and sold to a Black Country scrap yard during the following February. *Paul Leavens*.

(*below*) The Southern Region seemed loathe to apply shed plates to the BR Standard Cl.2s as exhibited here by Ramsgate based No.84029 running bunker first through Margate station circa 1958. *Paul Leavens*.

No.84001 working a Liverpool (Lime Street) to Manchester (Oxford Road) via Warrington (Bank Quay, Low Level) all stations passenger service on 14th April 1962, Dallam based Cl.2 No.84001 pauses at about mid-day at the latter station during its somewhat leisurely journey between the two Lancashire cities. This service was in its final months of operation and the recently acquired Cl.2MT would soon be laid up at 8B until another transfer – its last – took the six-coupled tank to Llandudno Junction shed in time for Christmas. Prior to its short sojourn at Warrington Dallam, No.84001 had worked from Crewe, Bolton, Wrexham, and Birkenhead; each location offered work but the changing traffic patterns and lack of traffic saw the engine and her sisters continually losing work and being stored. It would be interesting to see the true mileage compared with the expected mileage for these engines. *David Dalton.*

(*above*) No.84011 laid-up at Fleetwood in May 1965 shortly after withdrawal. *Chris Dunne*.

(*below*) No.84006 and 84005 dumped at J.Buttigieg's yard in Newport, Monmouthshire. This particular scrap merchant purchased six of the class including our subjects here. Withdrawn 30th October 1965, No.84006 was sold in January and arrived in Newport on 7th January with sister 84005 both ex Leicester shed They were reported as still intact during a visit in August. Note the motion still in place! *Chris Dunne*.

12: CLASS 9F 2-10-0

Eastern Region – The ER became a major recipient of the 9F 2-10-0 with no less than eighty-five engines being sent new to six different sheds between May 1954 and December 1958. The depots involved were: Annesley (2); Darnall (1); Doncaster (39); March (10); Mexborough (2); New England (31). Within weeks of delivery three of the sheds, those with the lowest number of engines received, had all lost their initial allocation to Doncaster. But over the years the ER allocation changed slightly with March giving up its 9Fs to New England or Annesley by June 1957, the latter building up its own stud for those coal train workings to Woodford and beyond during the depot's transition from Eastern Region to Midland Region control. Doncaster held on to its batches until most of them were withdrawn somewhat prematurely starting in 1964 but some managed to 'survive' until 1966. New England too had a short affair with its 9Fs but many were transferred away before the chop but they too became early casualties no matter which ER depot they went to. It appears that the Eastern Region was on a mission to rid itself of every steam locomotive it possessed as soon as possible. The year 1965 sticks out as one of the craziest in BR's history as no less than sixty-six 9Fs – just over a quarter of the class – were withdrawn; 1964 had already seen fifteen of them condemned. 1967 also stood out with one hundred and three withdrawn but it was now the eve of the end and such numbers would be expected. So now we ask ourselves why BR built so many Standard locomotives knowing full well that all of them would not work for anywhere near the accepted and expected 30-plus years in revenue earning service.

No.92014 at Stratford in July 1954 after its attendance at the Willesden International Railway Congress Exhibition in June! Since then the engine had been in traffic for a couple of weeks and that 'exhibition finish' was now disappearing under a coat of road dirt, never to be repeated! Curiously No.92014 has yet to acquire a shed plate which at this time would have been 31B March but it may well have been 'between sheds' and was awaiting a 30A Stratford plate, its next abode? *Paul Leavens.*

Leaving Wood Green station in its wake, New England's No.92141 heads for home with an afternoon mixed freight on Saturday 7th October 1961! New to 34E in July 1957, 92141 ended its days at Colwick transferring there in October 1965 from Langwith Junction. It never worked during the short time it was able at Colwick and was condemned in December. *Paul Leavens*.

The crew of No.92145, another New England charge, peer at the photographer installed at Wood Green on that same Saturday 7th October 1961. Their train consists of empty open wagons used for the transportation of bricks from the London Brick Co. brickyards and kilns at Peterborough to London and other points south. Being a Saturday afternoon, this train has a good chance of reaching Peterborough before dark. *Paul Leavens*.

All the tender details are there: BR1F No.1180 of 1955, 5625 gallons capacity. The welded and riveted tender coupled to Doncaster bound No.92091 at Swindon in November 1956. Note the loose coupling attached for works use with the screw coupling behind. The old lion and wheel emblem would not be superseded for another eight months. No.92091 became one of the rarities amongst Doncaster's allocation in that it worked into the final year of steam, being withdrawn from Carnforth in May 1968. Although 36A had this engine initially, it was soon reallocated to Annesley where it worked from March 1957 to July 1965 when it transferred to Speke Junction. *Paul Leavens*.

(*above*) This undated image of No.92187 departing from Doncaster station with an Up working is included to reveal some top-side detail of an in-service 9F coupled with a BR1F tender. The coal in the tender leaves a lot to be desired but that was one of the reasons for the building of the BR Standards – to burn the inferior coal on offer! *SVMRC*.

(*below*) One of Doncaster's 1958 batch – 92176 – meanders along the Up slow south of Doncaster station and is about to pass beneath St James' bridge with a fitted freight in August 1959. *SVMRC*.

(*above*) New England's No.92181 heads south through Potters Bar with a load of coal for London in 1959. This engine was new to the Peterborough shed in November 1957 and the chances are that it was never cleaned except after works attention. One of those 9Fs which remained loyal to 35A, No.92181 was withdrawn from there in February 1965 – just seven years and four months old! *SVMRC.*

(*below*) No.92172 – you'll have to take our word for that – moves away from the signal on the Down slow just south of St James' bridge, Doncaster circa 1960 with a train of building bricks from Peterborough. An A3 approaches with an express on the Down fast whilst a trio of K3s and a B1 have business in the Garden carriage sidings. The 9F spent the whole of its short life – January 1958 to April 1966 – allocated to Doncaster Carr shed. *SVMRC.*

(*above*) New England's No.92141 departs from New England yards and joins the main line to the south with a fitted freight for London in July 1960. The atrocious external condition of 34E's charges is evident from this vantage point. Goods installations such as that depicted here are now a thing of the past. It's amazing that in less than fifty years a whole industry can be virtually swept away! *SVMRC*.

(*below*) Propelling its brake van, No.92144 heads back to Langwith Junction shed on Friday 12th February 1965. Note the bridge which inadvertently inspired hundreds if not thousands or more homes to be covered with stone cladding! *Paul Leavens*.

London Midland Region – Taking the lion's share of the class with 100 engines allocated initially to seven sheds, the LMR's lot was to swell considerably over the fourteen years from the introduction of the 9F to withdrawal. No.92008 became the first of the LM batch and along with sister 92009 it was allocated to Wellingborough which incidentally took in the largest slice of the class, when new, at forty-one examples. Nos.92015 to 92029 was also sent to 15A and that group included all of the controversial Crosti-boilered engines 92020-92029. The next batch – 92045 to 92049 were also sent to Wellingborough, arriving during February and March 1955 but then after a break of five months, Toton got its first lot when Nos.92050 to 92059 emerged from Crewe from August 1955 onwards. Wellingborough then received, on loan from November and December 1955, Nos.92060 to 92066 which were destined for the North Eastern Region but were not yet complete in every respect for their role working from Tyne Dock shed – their Westinghouse compressed air equipment was still being delivered – so the works at Crewe set them to work on the LMR rather than have them stored. It was during April and May 1956 that those 9Fs were eventually delivered to the NER. By that time Toton was having another batch delivered in the shape of Nos.92077 to 92081 which were helping to eliminate the Beyer Garratt 2-6-0-0-6-2s from 18A. Following on from Toton's lot Wellingborough got another five – 92082 to 92086. Resuming from 92100 to 92104 went to Toton whilst 92105 to 92108 were taken in by 15A. In October 1956 92109 and 92110 went to Toton but then the next pair deviated from the usual Midland Lines practice and went to Cricklewood becoming the first of the class to be shedded in London from new. Another shed to receive new 9Fs was Westhouses which welcomed Nos.92113 to 92120 during the Christmas and New Year period of 1956 and 1957. As if to seemingly hog further examples of the 2-10-0s, Wellingborough took in Nos.92121 to 92127 during February and March 1957. Solitary No.92128 went to Toton. Then came the first move away from the Midland main artery when Saltley, albeit a former Midland Railway motive power depot, received Nos.92129 to 92139 during the spring of 1957 (No.92136 was one of the few 9Fs which remained at one depot throughout its life – Saltley). No.92150 to 92167 became the last of the new engines to go directly to LMR sheds with Saltley, Toton, Wellingborough, and Westhouses all getting some but two new depots received one each: Kettering No.92163 and Leicester Midland No.92164. That wasn't the end of it concerning LM sheds though as re-allocations took place continuously over the years up to the elimination of steam on BR. Other depots which provided homes for the 9Fs included Barrow Hill, Bidston, Birkenhead, Bolton, Bromsgrove, Burton-on-Trent, Carnforth, Kingmoor, Kirkby-in-Ashfield, Newton Heath, Northampton, Rowsley, Speke Junction, Warrington Dallam, and Willesden. Former LMR sheds which became WR property and ex-WR shed which in turn became LMR property and which were associated with the 9Fs have been left out of the list. Some 145 BR Standard 9F 2-10-0s ended their days working from pure LM Region depots.

Another load of coal for London! Wellingborough's No.92083 runs through Tring on the Up slow on 11th May 1963 headed for the capital. *Paul Leavens.*

(*above*) We've read so much about the BR Standard 9F 2-10-0s being used on passenger trains, particularly excursions that we thought we might come across an image of such a working. We didn't, on the LMR at least but see later. However we have the next best thing an image of a 9F on a LMR shed where it has obviously worked into the nearest station on a passenger train and is complete with a headboard of sorts. No.92132 is at Blackpool North shed in September 1959 and is even basking in the early afternoon sunshine. At the time the 2-10-0 was allocated to Wellingborough so was possibly responsible for bringing in a train from Leicester and southwards or thereabouts that very morning. *D.H.Beecroft, Book Law collection.*

(*below*) Wellingborough's No.92019 stabled outside one of the Cricklewood roundhouses in 1956. Two of the 15A engines – including this one – were transferred to Cricklewood in December 1957 but Nos.92018 and 92019 were back at Wellingborough during January for what must have been one of the shortest 9F residences at any shed. An even shorter stay was performed by No.92159 which came from 15A in December 1958 and returned later in the month! No.92014 was transferred to Cricklewood from Toton for a more respectable three months from July to October 1961 but it was sent then to Annesley. No.92057 was another which came to 14A residing from May 1960 to October 1961; No.92057 too was sent to Annesley. However before all of them came, Nos.92111 and 92112 – new in November 1956 – arrived and were joined by sisters 92108 and 92110 immediately afterwards. No.92119 completed the quintet in January 1959 but they had all gone by April 1959 when Wellingborough beckoned. *Paul Leavens.*

No.92020 laid-up at Wellingborough for numerous reasons it would appear! Fitted with a smoke deflector over the final chimney, this was the ultimate version of the Crosti engines' before conversion to conventional type boilers. This particular engine was stored from May 1959 to March 1961 prior to being taken to Crewe for conversion. *Paul Leavens*.

Four of the Crosti engines stored at Wellingborough with No.92021 prominent. *Paul Leavens*.

(*above*) All is forgiven! Leaving the MSW electrified lines behind, recently de-Crosti'ed No.92020 heads south through Woodhouse on the south-eastern quadrant of Sheffield with a fitted freight on a sunny morning during the late summer in 1961. *SVMRC*.

(*below*) Before the wires went up! Toton's No.92153 runs through the deep cutting at Tring with a mixed freight on Saturday 20th July 1963. *Paul Leavens*.

(*above*) Annesley's No.92067 runs north with returning coal empties and is about to enter the southern portal of Catesby tunnel on the old GCR main line on 22nd May 1963. *Paul Leavens*.

(*below*) On the same day another Annesley 9F – No.92069 – runs south with an Up mineral train, one of the 'Annesley Runners' heading for Woodford yard with another load of coal for Greater London. *Paul Leavens*.

(*above*) Whilst working an Up freight from Carlisle, Toton's No.92077 encounters a slight grade at Ais Gill on 20th August 1963. *Paul Leavens*.

(*below*) It doesn't look like much of a load but the continuous welded rail on the special bogie flats behind Newton Heath's No.92208 constituted a lot of weight requiring a banker on the climb up to Shap summit. The train had originated at Castleton P.W. depot near Rochdale and the 9F was en route to its new home at Kingmoor – albeit a few weeks late. This was one of those rare instances when BR co-ordinated two separate moves into one! *Paul Leavens*.

The cold morning of 28th September 1963 sees Toton 9F No.92075 making plenty of steam in Hatch End as it departs from London with coal empties for the East Midlands pits. *Paul Leavens*.

(*above*) Toton's No.92048 joins the usual crowd at Willesden on 21st June 1964. Note that Toton's former 18A shed code had changed to 16A, as and from September 1963. *Paul Leavens*.

(*below*) Loyal to the end! Saltley's No.92136 heads for home with a fitted freight through Chesterfield in 1961. This engine was allocated to 21A from being new in June 1957 to withdrawal in October 1966. *SVMRC*.

(*above*) Stranger in town! Ex-Crosti No.92028 awaits the signal at Southall on 9th June 1965 when it was allocated to Banbury shed for four months from March 1965. *Paul Leavens*.

(*below*) The former L&NWR shed at Northampton plays host to Toton's No.92156 in September 1959 shortly after the 9F had returned from the works at Crewe where a Casual Light repair had been given along with a thorough clean and some specific painting. Resident Cl.5 No.45292 rests in the background. *Paul Leavens*.

(*above*) Inside one of Wellingborough's roundhouses with resident No.92125 having some work done on its cylinders. Note that the 2-10-0 had to be parted from its tender for this operation which took place during March 1960. No.92101's tender is also standing alone; no doubt No.92101 is also getting some attention from the fitters at 15A. It would be interesting to know why No.92125's tender is not positioned the correct way round to be coupled with the engine when the time arrives! *Paul Leavens.*

(*below*) Resplendent in BR period filth, resident No.92110 stables at Wellingborough shed in August 1959. *Paul Leavens.*

North Eastern Region – The NER had a rather modest number of 9Fs allocated compared with the three larger regions and to keep things even more specific, the ten engines chosen were destined to work just one type of traffic on one particular route. The engines, all Crewe built arrived in two batches thus: 92060 to 92066 between April and May 1956 and 92097 to 92099 during June and July 1956. In reality the former batch should have been entrenched at Tyne Dock during November and December 1955 but shortage of materials – the all-important air pumps – delayed their allocation to the North-East; their interim employment is related to under the LMR notes. The NE Region in general had little use for the 2-10-0s being self-sufficient in eight-coupled freight locomotives but as these older engines were withdrawn, some 9Fs migrated to York and the former Lancashire & Yorkshire engine shed at Wakefield – which became NE Region property in the mid-1950s – also had use for a few of the class. The Tyne Dock 'ten' started to be withdrawn in May 1965 when No.92066 went for scrap but the rest remained in employment until mid and late 1966 when diesels took over the iron ore workings. The last of them actually went in April 1967 because No.92065 was re-allocated to Wakefield in November 1966.

No.92097 was the first of a batch of three – 92097-92099 – sent to Tyne Dock shed during the summer of 1956 to finish off their requirements for 9F haulage of the Tyne Dock-Consett iron ore trains where the specially fitted Westinghouse air pumps were used to open and close the bogie hopper wagon doors. As mentioned elsewhere, similarly fitted Nos.92060 to 92066 were somewhat late being allocated to 52H but by May 1956 they were all in residence and working the ore trains. The 2-10-0 is stabled on a stub of track awaiting a call down to Dock Bottom where a loaded train will be waiting for the 9Fs services for the run to Consett. The date has been lost but the late 1950s would not be too far off the mark. *Paul Leavens*.

(*above*) No.92061 eases through Pelaw with a load of ore for Consett ironworks on 15th April 1965. An unidentified English Electric Type 4 diesel-electric from Gateshead shed waits for the train to pass at which point it will follow the ensemble up the grade for the next couple of miles until the gradient requires the train to seek assistance over the 1 in 49 and steeper sections of the route for the following six miles to Annfield. *Paul Leavens*.

(*below*) Beyond Pelaw and it's beginning to bite as 92061 and the 2,000 horsepower banker head west. *Paul Leavens*.

When the 9Fs became anybody's to work as they wished:

Hauling a long rake of empty hoppers and 16-ton mineral wagons, what appears to be York's No.92206 heads east through the Calder valley near Mirfield on a cold Saturday 19th November 1966. This engine was actually a Wakefield charge at this time having transferred from 50A to 56A during October. Prior to its regional transfer to York from Feltham in September 1963, this 9F had started its operational career on the WR at Bristol's St Philips Marsh shed. Then to Bath Green Park for the summer of 1960, then Westbury for the winter before a move to the Southern at Eastleigh in January 1961 working oil trains from Fawley. It was condemned at Wakefield in May 1967 aged eight years! *Paul Leavens*.

(*above*) Being followed by a diesel shunter on a trip working to Kingmoor yard, No.92208 crosses the River Eden at Etterby and approaches Kingmoor engine shed on 6th April 1966. Starting its BR career at Laira in June 1959 with 92209, this 9F departed the West Country during the following March – 92208 had transferred to Canton in August 1959 – moving to Southall. In December 1961 it followed its sister to Cardiff and managed a stint at Canton and East Dock before moving to Newton Heath and finally Carlisle where it stretched its lifespan a little bit more than some others in the class being withdrawn in November 1966. *Paul Leavens*.

(*below*) The southern approach to Kingmoor yard as seen from the main-line connections for Kingmoor engine shed on 6th April 1966 with a rather smart No.92233 bringing a long van train for the yard. This 9Fs future did not finish in Carlisle and in January 1968 it was transferred to Speke Junction where it was withdrawn upon arrival! However, it was one of the few which made it into 1968 albeit for just a few weeks. *Paul Leavens*.

No.92239 had apparently been allocated to Eastleigh shed since July 1961, initially on loan but permanently later in the month; in May 1963 it moved on to Feltham and later that summer to York. However, this image of Eastleigh shed reveals sister No.92248 stabled on Saturday 28th October 1961 when that 9F was on Cardiff Canton's register. This engine had probably worked from Newport, South Wales on a return oil empties to Fawley which was to be established as an Eastleigh duty but at this date 71A did not have enough 9Fs to cover all the oil workings from Fawley for which they had been reallocated from the Midland and Western regions from December 1960 on loan and then from January 1961 on a permanent basis. By October 1961 the following 9Fs were allocated to Eastleigh: 92205; 92206; 92211; 92231; and 92239. The 2-10-0s could handle the 1,200 ton trains from Millbrook yard – originating at Fawley refinery and worked to the yard by a pair of tank locomotives – to Birmingham with relative ease and later took in other destinations. The introduction of diesel locomotives on the working basically stemmed the use of further 9Fs being allocated to Eastleigh. For the record the three 71A 9Fs all migrated to Feltham in May 1963 and then to York in September 1963. Note the ex-WR Pannier tanks stabled after works attention. *Paul Leavens*.

(*above*) Kingmoor 9F No.92233 again and heading towards Leeds (City) on a mucky 9th October 1966 with a five coach express from Carlisle. Passing Wortley junction, where the former North Eastern Railway roundhouse is just visible in the murk. *Paul Leavens*.

(*below*) Another passenger train, or at least passenger stock, being 9F hauled. We are in the Scottish Region now at Beattock on 1st August 1964 with Kingmoor's newly acquired and very leaky No.92249 topping the bank with what appears to be a train of condemned stock destined perhaps to one of those scrapyards found in Scotland's Central Belt. *Paul Leavens*.

Western Region – The WR was the first region to receive the BR Standard 9F 2-10-0s – they were also the last – with Nos.92000 to 92004 being officially allocated to Newport's Ebbw Junction shed during January 1954. Nos.92005, 92006 and 92007 followed in February. That's how it looked on paper but reality was completely different! It took a while for the authorities to sort things out but things did get better once a few misunderstandings had been ironed out and some adjustments made to the engines. The Western did not get any more 9Fs until Crewe provided Nos.92221 to 92250 between April and December 1958. Why it took an interval of four years for the region to accept any more of the 2-10-0s is unknown to this writer but no doubt someone would have made a note of the reason(s). The first ten of that 1958 batch, Nos.92221 to 92230 were sent to Banbury where their prowess was welcomed for working the locally provided iron-ore trains in particular. However they didn't all stay long with just a couple of the original batch putting some time in; engines from later batches made up the numbers and added to the variety. Laira got five of the Banbury engines in June 1959 and even though they all moved away in March 1960, three of them returned in June to finish off the summer season. Half of that first batch of Banbury 9Fs remained on the WR to be withdrawn there whilst the others had moved away to the LM and ER. The next half dozen – 92231 to 92236 – were allocated to Pontypool Road during August and September. They too did some roaming during their short lives with LM sheds receiving some of them prior to withdrawal whilst the Southern had use of 92231s (see SR notes) services. Newport Ebbw Junction once again received some Crewe built examples but this time Nos.92237 to 92244 and 92248 and 92249 were better received even though the first five transferred to: Canton (1) and Old Oak Common (4) almost immediately. Nos 92245 to 92247 went to 81A in time for Christmas 1958 whilst Banbury received Crewe's final adventure in steam – the 7,331st steam locomotive. After four months No.92250 was loaned to the steam locomotive testing station at Rugby from April to September when – after thirty-odd 'runs' – its double chimney was replaced by a Giesl Oblong Ejector experimental chimney for a series of eighty-four tests 'runs' when it was found that fuel savings were made. No.92250 kept the Giesl ejector for the rest of its life but no other BR locomotive except BB No.34064 was similarly equipped. The Western Regions final batch of 9Fs came from Swindon and these proved to be not only the last WR steam locomotives but BR's too. Nos.92203 to 92220 were put into traffic at a painfully slow rate between April 1959 and March 1960 which equates roughly to one every three weeks! Delaying the inevitable? Nothing as romantic! It was mainly down to division of resources whereby the men who built the locomotives were diverted to getting diesels into traffic rather than these no longer necessary steam giants. It would appear to be churlish to point out that six of those eighteen Swindon built engines for the WR survived into preservation whereas none of the thirty-five built by Swindon for the ER survive!

No.92002 stands in a siding at Swindon awaiting works attention on 28th March 1954. The works at Swindon was rather slow as regards commissioning locomotives built off the WR be that they came from private contractors or other BR workshops. This 9F was a creation from an alien world and would be treated as such until somebody came to their senses. The Great Western Railway – sorry Western Region – was still running as a completely separate entity to the rest of British Railways it seemed to some and the BR Standard 9Fs were at this time becoming the punch bags of a truly unimaginative, set-in-stone, stubborn organisation which refused to see good in anything which was not built at Swindon! Note that No.92002 still had no shed plate. What next? *Paul Leavens*.

(*above*) No.92001 new outside the paint shop at Crewe works in January 1954. This engine – along with 92002 – went to Manchester in January to the former Great Central locomotive works at Gorton as part of the running-in regime but the real reason for their visit was to use the weighing facilities which were apparently superior to the Crewe set-up. On 2nd February the same pair departed Crewe for Ebbw Junction shed via Swindon shops where WR ATC was fitted. The story of those first 9Fs being accepted in South Wales was not a pretty one and no doubt local misguided loyalties played a part in the various minor 'faults' which occurred during the first six months of their residency. *David Dalton.*

(*below*) The left side of 92001; the January murk does little to enhance the image but you get the idea! *David Dalton.*

Helping the enemy! EVENING STAR works a freight carrying new commercial road vehicles through Oxford station on 16th March 1963. No.92220 was allocated to Oxford shed from October 1962 – ex Old Oak Common – to August 1963 when it transferred to Bath Green Park for its final summer season on the Somerset & Dorset. You couldn't make this up but 'Castle' No.7029 CLUN CASTLE is preparing to set off in the opposite direction also towards preservation. *Paul Leavens*.

(*above*) Rolling south through the junction at Hatton and past milepost 112/1, Saltley based No.92135 has charge of a mixed freight circa 1960. *SVMRC.*

(*below*) Banbury based No.92204 runs through Wolvercot on 17th May 1963 with a short pick-up freight consisting mainly Presflo bulk powder wagons recovered from the Blue Circle cement works at nearby Bletchington. That such a large motive power asset as a 9F was used for local pick-up work seems to be a waste of resources but BR became very good at that! *Paul Leavens.*

No.92204 again with the same pick-up job but on the following day! *Paul Leavens.*

Heading south along the S&D main line at Bath near Bridge Road, No.92220 EVENING STAR has charge of a somewhat lightweight stopping train in August 1963. The by now rather dirty but still special 2-10-0 did two seasons working over the Somerset & Dorset line from Bath Green Park shed; July to September 1962 and August to October 1963. After this stint it was off to Cardiff East Dock shed where it worked its last revenue earning jobs for BR. Withdrawn in March 1965 it was put into 'WR Store' to await preservation but that store seemed to include any available siding because this writer saw the 9F on a stub of line opposite Pontypool Road engine shed during 1966 looking decidedly vandalised! *Paul Leavens.*

(*above*) Another 9F hauled passenger train on the S&D at Bath but this time No.92245 is in charge of a Bournemouth-Bath working. Note that the dirt was not reserved purely for 92220. The tablet catcher can be seen just below the cab door, affixed to the tender. Yes, No.92245 is also one of the preserved examples. *Paul Leavens*.

(*below*) Destined for Ebbw Junction shed at Newport, double-chimney No.92242 stands on the yard at Crewe South shed in October 1958 during its running-in trials. The last of the Crewe built engines and indeed the last steam locomotive built at Crewe – 92250, also destined for the WR – was put into traffic just a couple of months after this scene was captured on film. *Paul Leavens*.

(*above*) Lickey banker No.92079 stands outside the works at Swindon in 1959 awaiting entry to the shops for a Casual Heavy overhaul. The 9F actually spent some 202 weekdays out of service at Swindon from 15th May 1959 to 4th January 1960. But it was repaired and returned to service at Bromsgrove where it worked from May 1956 to October 1963 when sister 92223 took over the job for three months before it was condemned. Then 92230 took up the mantle until the summer of 1964 when the diesels arrived. Bromsgrove shed closed in September 1964 and banking thereafter was only performed on freight trains. Meanwhile, what stood-in for 92079 during its long absence at Swindon? Initially Saltley provided No.92135 but being a WR duty by now No.92231 from Canton quickly replaced the 21A engine; 92005 also did a stint on the bank. The 'Brit' is No.70028 ROYAL STAR. *Paul Leavens*.

(*below*) Further evidence of 9Fs being used for passenger workings other than excursion trains! This is Old Oak Common's No.92246 standing at the head of an express at Paddington in 1960. Where the train was destined is, like the date, unknown. *Paul Leavens*.